D1525275

College Football's Most Memorable Games,
1913 Through 1990

To my wife Arlene and son Eric
for their support
—F. E.

Thanks to JFK for providing inspiration
to make a difference
—E. B. S.

College Football's Most Memorable Games, 1913 Through 1990

*The Stories of 54
History-Making Contests*

by Fred Eisenhammer
and Eric B. Sondheimer

McFarland & Company, Inc., Publishers
Jefferson, North Carolina, and London

British Library Cataloguing-in-Publication data are available

Library of Congress Cataloguing-in-Publication Data

Eisenhammer, Fred.
    College football's most memorable games, 1913 through 1990 : the
stories of 54 history-making contests / by Fred Eisenhammer and Eric
B. Sondheimer.
        p.   cm.
    Includes bibliographical references and index. ∞
    ISBN 0-89950-656-9 (lib. bdg. : 50# alk. paper)
    1. Football—United States—History—20th century.   2. College
sports—United States—History—20th century.   I. Sondheimer, Eric
B. II. Title.
GV950.E47   1992
796.332′63′0973—dc20   92-50303
                                                                            CIP

Manufactured in the United States of America

McFarland & Company, Inc., Publishers
  Box 611, Jefferson, North Carolina 28640

Acknowledgments

Information for this book was obtained from football media guides and sports information departments of the following universities:

Alabama
Army
Boston College
Brigham Young
California
Chicago
Clemson
Colorado
Columbia
Harvard
Iowa
Louisiana State
Miami
Michigan
Michigan State
Navy
Nebraska

Notre Dame
Ohio State
Penn State
Princeton
Rice
Southern Methodist
Stanford
Syracuse
Texas
Texas A&M
Texas Christian
University of California at
    Los Angeles
University of Southern
    California
Wisconsin

Many thanks to all the sports information directors and their assistants who fielded our many questions and requests.

Table of Contents

Introduction

Near the end of the 1966 football season, Michigan State played host to Notre Dame in what the media billed as "The Game of the Decade." Indeed, the game had all the ingredients of a classic college football matchup. Notre Dame, ranked No. 1 in the country, was outscoring opponents by an average of 38-4. Second-ranked Michigan State was outscoring opponents by a margin of 31-10.

The Irish rallied from a 10-0 deficit to finish in a 10-10 tie, but the game ended on a controversial note. Notre Dame Coach Ara Parseghian decided to keep the ball on the ground and run out the clock with 1:30 remaining and Notre Dame in possession at its 35-yard line.

It was one of the most memorable games in college football history, but there have been many, many others.

Such well-known professional football players as Joe Montana, O. J. Simpson, Bobby Layne, Sammy Baugh, Jim Brown, Jim Plunkett and Jim McMahon played leading roles in some of college football's greatest games. But other players—whose names would only be remembered in the context of a single play—also played pivotal roles in memorable games.

For instance:

- In the 1929 Rose Bowl, Roy Riegels of Cal picked up a Georgia Tech fumble and raced 60 yards toward the wrong goal line and was downed at his team's one-yard line. For his monumental gaffe, he was tagged with a nickname that stuck: "Wrong Way" Riegels.
- In the 1939 Rose Bowl, two reserves from USC, quarterback Doyle Nave and end Al Krueger, combined on a 14-yard touchdown pass in the final minute to give the Trojans a stunning 7-3 victory over Duke, which had been undefeated, untied and unscored upon in its previous nine games.
- In the 1954 Cotton Bowl, Alabama's Tommy Lewis gained notoriety when he bolted from the sidelines to tackle Rice halfback Dicky Moegle

in the middle of what undoubtedly would have been a 95-yard touchdown run.

- In 1984, Gerald Phelan gave Boston College an improbable 47–45 victory over Miami when he caught a 65-yard desperation pass from Doug Flutie as time expired.

There are several ways a college football game typically can qualify to belong among the sport's most memorable.

A single electrifying play can catapult the game to national prominence. "Wrong Way" Riegels single-handedly made the game against Georgia Tech memorable. Cal, likewise, turned its annual "Big Game" against Stanford into a giant game in 1982. After Stanford took a 20–19 lead with four seconds remaining, Cal's ensuing kickoff return produced one of the most bizarre endings in history. The Bears lateraled five times on the return en route to scoring the winning touchdown, navigating through Stanford's team and Stanford's band, which had marched mindlessly onto the field believing the game had ended when Cal's third ball-carrier, Dwight Garner, appeared to be tackled.

Spectacular individual performances also can make a game memorable. In 1924, for instance, halfback Red Grange amassed 402 yards in total offense and scored five touchdowns in leading Illinois to a 39–14 victory over Michigan. Jim Brown, likewise, enjoyed a phenomenal effort in his final game for Syracuse. He set an NCAA Division I record by scoring 43 points against Colgate in 1956, scoring six touchdowns and kicking seven point-afters.

Spectacular comebacks also have made games special. The 1963 Rose Bowl was renowned for its tremendous finish. Wisconsin trailed USC, 42–14, early in the fourth quarter but rallied behind quarterback Ron VanderKelen before losing, 42–37. Some consider it the most exciting bowl game ever.

In 1974, USC put together a rousing comeback by scoring 55 points in 17 minutes to rally from a 24–0 deficit and shock Notre Dame, 55–24, behind Anthony Davis' four touchdowns in a truly fantastic finish. Maryland didn't take a backseat to anyone in comebacks when the Terrapins rallied from a seemingly insurmountable 31–0 halftime deficit to overcome Miami, 42–40, in 1984.

Huge upsets or stunning victories also have provided memorable games. An 18-point underdog against Oklahoma in 1957, Notre Dame snapped the Sooners' seven-game winning streak with a 7–0 victory — one year after Oklahoma had handed the Irish their worst-ever defeat (40–0) at home.

Certain games become more prominent because national ratings, perhaps even the No. 1 ranking, are involved. The buildup to the 1966 Michigan State–Notre Dame game was heightened because the No. 1 ranking hinged on the outcome. Thus, many bowl games oftentimes are elevated to the status of memorable because of their importance to national rankings.

National rankings, however, don't necessarily have to be at stake for a game to earn hallowed status. Harvard and Yale were both 8–0 but unranked in 1968 when they squared off for the Ivy League title. Yale opened a 29–13 lead, but Harvard scored 16 points in the final 42 seconds to finish in a 29–29 tie. The next day the *Harvard Crimson* student newspaper proudly announced: "HARVARD BEATS YALE, 29–29."

The national ratings became a regular feature in 1936 when the Associated Press introduced its weekly sportswriters and broadcasters top 20 poll. In 1950, United Press International came up with national rankings of its own, using votes by college football coaches.

College football games considered for this book were played in 1912 or later. It was in 1912 when football's modern-day rules were introduced, and football became the game as we know it today. Many of the modern-day rules applied directly to passing, which became legal only six years earlier. Passers in 1912 now could throw the ball for any distance and could use an additional ten-yard area past the goal line. Also in 1912, the number of downs was increased from three to four.

The Rutgers-Princeton game in 1869 has been cited as the first college football game, but the game, in fact, was played under conditions that were more similar to soccer. Players were not eligible to advance the ball with their hands, although they could kick it.

In 1913, Notre Dame demonstrated the potential of the passing game in a 35–13 conquest of powerful Army. Knute Rockne, who played end for Notre Dame and would later become a legendary Notre Dame coach, was one of the stars of that game.

Notre Dame has taken part in many memorable games over the years — a befitting role for a college with a reputation as a perennial national power. Other schools with rich football traditions such as USC and Alabama have also written their share of memorable football chapters.

For this book, more than 60 players and coaches who played a role in some of the greatest games in college football history were interviewed to provide insights and an updated look at some of these historic contests.

Notre Dame Passes
into a New Era
Notre Dame 35, Army 13 • November 1, 1913

Notre Dame launched a new era in college football by introducing a spectacular passing game never seen before.

Behind quarterback Gus Dorais and end Knute Rockne, Notre Dame threw caution—and many passes—to the wind in unleashing a wide-open offense that flattened and stunned powerful Army, 35–13, before 5,000 fans in West Point, New York.

Army entered the game as the premier passing team in the East. But Army used the pass sparingly, as a last-resort, desperation move. Notre Dame, on the other hand, demonstrated against Army that the pass could be used as a springboard to victory.

Dorais, Notre Dame's 145-pound, tremendously agile quarterback, frustrated Army with his long passes, including a 40-yard heave to Rockne, the longest pass ever completed to that day. All told, Dorais completed 14 of 17 passes for 243 yards and two touchdowns. He misfired on his first two passes before embarking on his amazing string of accuracy.

Rockne, the left end, Fred Gushurst, the right end, and Joe Pliska, the left halfback, took turns playing catch with Dorais. And when a thoroughly confused Army team tried to adjust to Notre Dame's revolutionary offense, fullback Ray Eichenlaub bulled his way for sizable gains on the ground. Eichenlaub scored two of Notre Dame's three touchdowns in the fourth quarter when Notre Dame turned its 14–13 lead into a rout.

Notre Dame caught Army by surprise with its blitzkrieg passing attack. Rockne noticed this fact early as Army stood prepared to shut down Notre Dame's ground game.

"Their guards and tackles went tumbling into us to stop (our) line

bucks and plunges," Rockne said. "Instead, Dorais stepped neatly back and flipped the ball to an uncovered end or halfback."[1]

Rockne caught a 25-yard touchdown pass from Dorais in the first quarter to give Notre Dame a 7–0 lead after Eichenlaub and Pliska had brought the ball downfield with successful runs. Army, though, rallied to score two consecutive second-quarter touchdowns to take a 13–7 lead, but that only heightened Notre Dame's resolve.

Notre Dame, coached by Jesse Harper, responded with an 85-yard touchdown drive in the second quarter to take the lead for good. Dorais completed long passes to Rockne and Pliska to set up the touchdown, scored by Pliska on the ground. Dorais threw a five-yard strike to Pliska in the fourth quarter for his final touchdown pass.

Dorais' passing moves were no surprise to Rockne. The two had worked diligently on perfecting their patterns the previous summer when they worked as lifeguards at the beach resort of Cedar Point, Ohio.

Although Notre Dame's offense drew most of the raves, its over-shadowed defense also turned in its share of heroics. Notre Dame made several outstanding defensive stands, its biggest coming in the third quarter when Notre Dame was clinging to a 14–13 lead. Using runs by Paul Hodgson, Leland Hobbs and Frank Milburn, Army drove to Notre Dame's two-yard line from where the Cadets had first and goal.

But after two runs resulted in losses, Army quarterback Vernon Prichard lofted a desperation pass to Louis Merillat in the end zone, but the pass was intercepted by Dorais. It was all Notre Dame after that.

Even Army's final touchdown in the second quarter came despite a brilliant goal-line stand by Notre Dame. After failing to score on three runs from the Notre Dame one-yard line, Army picked up a first down by penalty. With a fresh set of downs, Army still had trouble scoring, needing three more plays before Prichard plowed in for a touchdown to give Army a 13–7 lead.

Notre Dame had tuned up for Army by posting victories of 87–0 against Ohio Northern, 20–7 against South Dakota, and 62–0 against Alma. Despite losing only one game in its previous four seasons, Notre

Opposite: The completion of one of the startling Dorais to Rockne passes which beat Army in 1913 and modified the entire game of football. Here's Knute making a touchdown. (Photo courtesy of Notre Dame Sports Information Department.)

Dame had entered the game as a decided underdog and was considered nothing more than a regional power. After its resounding victory, Notre Dame earned the status of national power.

Postscript: Notre Dame's stunning formula for victory revolutionized college football. The pass became recognized as an important and a potentially integral part of a team's offense. More and more teams worked to incorporate the passing game in their offensive philosophies. The forward pass had become legalized in 1906, but only in 1912 had many of the passing game's restrictions been eased, allowing for example, a pass to be thrown for any distance. The passing game's potential was demonstrated for the first time in Notre Dame's victory over Army.

"The press and the football public hailed this new game," said Rockne about the pass, "and Notre Dame received credit as the originator of a style of play that we simply systematized."[2]

Army reserve and president-to-be Dwight Eisenhower watched disconsolately from the bench during the Cadets' loss to Notre Dame, Army's lone defeat of the season. The Cadets won their remaining four games, to finish 8–1. Notre Dame won its remaining three games to finish 7–0 in Harper's first season as head coach.

Rockne was named head coach of Notre Dame in 1918, replacing Harper, who had led Notre Dame to a 34-5-1 record in his five seasons. Rockne's teams won six national championships in his 13 years as Notre Dame coach. His winning percentage was a brilliant .881 (105-12-5), still college football's top mark. Rockne was killed in a plane crash in 1931 at 43.

Eichenlaub was named to the National Football Foundation's College Hall of Fame and Rockne and Harper were selected to the National Football Foundation's Hall of Fame for college coaches.

References

1. *Notre Dame 1990 Football Press Guide.*
2. Ibid.

Princeton Holds on with Dramatic Goal-Line Stand

Princeton 21, Chicago 18 • October 28, 1922

During this clash of the nation's titans, Princeton wiped out an 11-point deficit in the fourth quarter to score a 21–18 upset over the University of Chicago. But Princeton needed a dramatic goal-line stand with less than a minute remaining to preserve the victory before 32,000 fans at Stagg Field in Chicago.

Chicago, which had squandered an 18–7 lead at the end of three quarters, drove to Princeton's six-yard line with two minutes remaining in the game and trailing by three points. Running back John Thomas already had scored three touchdowns for Chicago and a fourth would give the Maroons the victory.

Chicago's powerful line plunges had consistently gained sizable yardage, but this time Princeton's defense would bend only slightly.

Thomas carried on first down, gaining three yards and moving the ball to Princeton's three-yard line. On second down, Thomas carried again — gaining a yard. On third and goal from the two, Thomas was stopped one yard short of the goal line.

Then on fourth down, Thomas got the call one final time. But Harland "Pink" Baker knifed into the backfield to tackle Thomas for a three-yard loss — the only time Thomas had lost yardage in the game.

Princeton's Jack Cleaves then punted the ball away from danger as time expired.

Princeton lineman Don Griffin said in 1991 that his team was fortunate that Chicago's timing was off on its final goal-line plays. "We took credit for stopping them, but the truth is that their plays were messed up," Griffin said. "There was so much yelling and screaming going on and Chicago's linemen didn't shift properly. This was the time before the huddle system and they were calling the signals loud and clear supposedly.

"It was so emotional at the end that we thought we had won the Harvard and Yale games in the same afternoon at Chicago," recalled Griffin.

Griffin made two of the tackles during the memorable goal-line stand to help Princeton improve to 5–0. Chicago, coached by Amos Alonzo Stagg, dropped to 3–1.

Chicago led, 12–7, at halftime behind backs John Thomas, Harry Thomas and Jim Pyott and appeared to have moved to an insurmountable 18–7 lead when John Thomas scored his third touchdown on a short run late in the third quarter.

Princeton was down, but not out at that point, Griffin said. "I think we were maybe befuddled but had not lost any spirit," he said. "We were outclassed as far as power was concerned because they had backs who could drive and pick up five yards every time they carried the ball."

Princeton may have been outmanned, but Coach Bill Roper's Tigers kept battling back.

Mired on its one-yard line early in the final period, Princeton got out of danger with a surprising 39-yard pass play from Cleaves to Johnny Gorman on a fake punt. Although the drive bogged down, Princeton was able to get field position for a punt that moved Chicago back to the Maroon 42.

One play after Chicago took over, a snap from center bounced off the shoulder of Chicago running back Willie Zorn. Princeton's Howdy Gray scooped up the rolling football and weaved his way 40 yards for the touchdown that allowed Princeton to cut its deficit to 18–14.

Griffin called Gray's touchdown the turning point of the game. "It was a case of missed signals. They had a new center and he made a bad pass," Griffin said. "It put us back in the game again."

Princeton now had the momentum. With five minutes remaining, Henry Crum plunged in from one yard out on fourth down for his second touchdown to cap a 58-yard march and the Tigers grabbed a 21–18 lead. A big play on the drive was a 25-yard pass play from Cleaves to Ken Smith.

The difference in the game?

Chicago missed on all three of its point-after attempts, while Smith, Princeton's left-footed kicker, made good on all three of his tries.

Postscript: After the dramatic victory, famed sportswriter Grantland Rice bestowed the tag, "Team of Destiny" on Princeton because in his opinion, the Tigers had only destiny going for them. Princeton started the season with only six experienced players, including All-American tackle Herb Treat, but fulfilled its destiny by defeating

Swarthmore, Harvard and Yale in its final three games to finish 8-0. It was the first time Princeton had gone undefeated and untied since 1903.

In December 1939, Chicago stunned the sports world by dropping football. The Maroons had won the Western Conference (Big Ten) title six times and had been coached for 41 years by Stagg (1892–1932), who pioneered the forward pass and the T-formation. Stagg coached for 57 years (1890 to 1946) at Springfield, Chicago and Pacific, and set a major-college record with 314 victories. The record remained until Alabama's Bear Bryant posted his 315th coaching victory in 1981. Chicago produced the first Heisman Trophy winner in halfback Jay Berwanger in 1935, but had fallen upon hard times in 1939 with such humiliating losses as 46–0 to Illinois, 61–0 to Ohio State and 85–0 to Michigan.

After the program was dropped, Chicago Coach Clark Shaughnessy moved on to the head coaching position at Stanford the following season and turned around the program in one miraculous year. Employing Shaughnessy's revolutionary T-formation, Stanford went 10-0, including a 21–13 victory over Nebraska in the Rose Bowl. The previous season, Stanford had gone 1-7-1.

Chicago resumed playing football in 1969, competing at the Division III level.

Illinois' Grange Runs
Up 402 Yards

Illinois 39, Michigan 14 • October 18, 1924

Red Grange, an All-American halfback from the University of Illinois, turned in an All-World performance against Michigan during the dedication game of Illinois' new $1,700,000 Memorial Stadium. Grange scored four touchdowns in the first quarter, five overall, and passed for a sixth as the Fighting Illini routed the Wolverines, 39–14.

In the first quarter alone, Grange piled up an astonishing 262 yards in total offense by shredding the Wolverines' defenders in a heart-stopping, broken-field style that turned the crowd of 67,000 fans into a cheering frenzy. Grange returned the opening kickoff 95 yards for a touchdown before zigzagging 67, 56, and 44 yards from the line of scrimmage for three more first-quarter scores. In the first 12 minutes, Grange tallied four touchdowns against a team that had allowed a total of four in two previous seasons.

After his fourth touchdown, Grange told trainer Matt Bullock that he was too exhausted to continue. Illinois Coach Bob Zuppke sent in Ray Gallivan to replace Grange. Gallivan played the second quarter as Grange rested, but in the second half, the 6-foot, 185-pound Grange continued his onslaught.

He ran ten yards for a touchdown in the third quarter and threw a 23-yard touchdown pass in the final quarter en route to 402 all-purpose yards, which included 64 yards in passing on six completions.

Grange turned this early-season showdown into a showcase of his brilliant abilities. Delighted Illini fans cheered wildly as Grange helped Illinois open a 27–0 lead at the end of the first quarter.

Michigan closed to within 27–7 at halftime, but Grange's third-quarter touchdown scamper put Illinois safely ahead at 33–7.

In a matchup of unbeaten teams from 1923, Michigan and Illinois, both 2-0 entering the game, had been rated even. But it was the Illini who were red-hot from the start.

Grange retrieved the opening kickoff from his five-yard line and veered to his left. He then cut to his right to elude a tackler and called on his 9.8-second 100-yard dash speed to sprint to the end zone.

"I remember very well starting down the middle with the opening kickoff, and then we had a pileup around the 35-yard line," said Grange in 1974. "I ran into a lot of traffic, and all of a sudden I was in the clear. It seemed to be that way the rest of the first quarter."[1]

The touchdown set the tone for the rest of the game.

Grange, a junior, repeatedly ran behind interference before bolting through an opening and then whirling around Michigan defensive backs. His elusive moves left Wolverine defenders shaking their heads in amazement.

"I don't think I ever played in any other game where every man did exactly what he was supposed to do," Grange said. "In the first quarter, if a man was supposed to block the end, he blocked the end. If he was supposed to hit the tackle, he hit the tackle."

"I don't think any college team in the nation could have licked us

Illinois halfback Red Grange. (Photo courtesy of Illinois Sports Information Department.)

on that day. Maybe on the Friday before or the Sunday afterward, they might have beat our brains in, but not on that one Saturday."[2]

There was considerable buildup to the game. The much-anticipated matchup of powerful football teams had been talked about throughout the summer of 1924 and even during the windup of baseball's pennant races. For the Midwest, this was going to be the game of the year. There was no love lost between Zuppke and his Michigan counterpart, Fielding H. "Hurry Up" Yost, the longtime Wolverine coach who also was the school's athletic director.

Zuppke informed his team by mail during the summer that Yost was taking the Illini lightly.

"Zup had worked on that game from the start of the summer," said Grange. "He started telling us all kinds of things Yost had been saying about us all summer. It wasn't until a long time afterward that I found out that Yost had been in Europe the whole summer.

"He had gotten us so riled up about Yost that we just couldn't lose."[3]

Postscript: Illinois won its next two games before finishing 8-1-1, losing only to Minnesota. The Illini, with Grange as their captain, were 5-3 the following season as Grange was named an All-American for the third consecutive year. He scored 31 touchdowns in 20 games for Illinois.

Michigan finished 6-2 with five shutouts. The Wolverines allowed only 54 points during the season, 39 to the Illini.

Grange, nicknamed the "Galloping Ghost" by sportswriter Grantland Rice, played seven seasons with the Chicago Bears of the National Football League. He played to huge crowds after signing in 1925 with Bears owner-coach George Halas, who expected that Grange would draw tremendous interest to his team and the NFL. Halas lined up an 18-game, coast-to-coast barnstorming tour that brought in crowds of 70,000 to New York's Polo Grounds and 75,000 to the Los Angeles Memorial Coliseum. Grange failed to reach contract terms with Halas for the 1926 season, so he bolted to the New York Yankees of the American Football League for that season. Grange suffered a serious knee injury during the 1927 season and did not play in 1928. He returned to the Bears in 1929 and played for Chicago through the 1934 season.

Although he enjoyed only moderate success as a professional, Grange was named to both the College and Pro Football Halls of Fame. He died in 1991 at 87.

References

1. Lon Eubanks, *The Fighting Illini — A Story of Illinois Football* (Huntsville, AL: The Strode Publishers, Inc., 1976).
2. Ibid.
3. Ibid.

Notre Dame Wins
One for "The Gipper"

Notre Dame 12, Army 6 • November 10, 1928

Notre Dame's 12–6 victory over heavily favored Army at Yankee Stadium before 78,188 fans was achieved in dramatic and emotional fashion both on and off the field.

It was both teams' seventh game of the season. Notre Dame entered the game at 4-2. Army was 6-0. Notre Dame was concerned about a possible sub-.500 finish with powerful Carnegie Tech and USC still left on its schedule. Army was making a strong bid for a national championship.

Recognizing the long odds of his team, Notre Dame Coach Knute Rockne assembled his team after their warm-up for the game and delivered a pep talk that provided his team with the equalizing ingredient: emotion.

When all was quiet in the looker room, Rockne slowly recounted his remembrances of George Gipp, Notre Dame's illustrious All-American halfback who died of complications from strep throat during his senior year in 1920. Gipp was Notre Dame's leading rusher and passer for three consecutive seasons beginning in 1918.

Rockne was at Gipp's bedside during Gipp's final days. Rockne related to his team Gipp's final wish: "'I've got to go, Rock. It's all right. I'm not afraid. Some time, Rock, when the team is up against it, when things are wrong and the breaks are beating the boys, tell them to go in there with all they've got and win just one for 'The Gipper.' I don't know where I'll be then, Rock. But I'll know about it, and I'll be happy.'"[1]

As Rockne talked, he knew his players were being moved. And he added, "The day before he died, Gipp asked me to wait until the situation seemed hopeless, then ask a Notre Dame team to go out and beat Army for him. This is the day, and you are the team."[2]

It was an oratorical bombshell, enervating Notre Dame like nothing else could. If the game was a mismatch on paper, Rockne knew he had just closed the odds.

"There was no one in the room that wasn't crying," line coach Ed

Haley said. "There was a moment of silence, and then all of a sudden those players ran out of the dressing room and almost tore the hinges off the door. They were all ready to kill someone."[3]

Notre Dame came out inspired, but Army also was ready to play. After a scoreless first half, Army took a 6–0 lead in the third quarter behind All-American halfback Chris Cagle, whose 25-yard run helped set up John Murrell for a two-yard touchdown run. Notre Dame then counterattacked. Later in the third quarter, halfback Jack Chevigny tied the score, 6–6, with a one-yard run on fourth down that capped a 64-yard march. After he scored, he picked himself off the ground and shouted, "That's one for 'The Gipper.'"[4]

Chevigny rallied Notre Dame again in the fourth quarter but was forced out of the game with an injury. No matter. Notre Dame would not be turned back this day. Rockne, in his 11th year as Notre Dame coach, replaced Chevigny with Bill Drew. Reserve Johnny O'Brien, a hurdler on the track team, came in to replace Johnny Colrick at left end.

With Notre Dame on Army's 32-yard line, left halfback Butch Niemiec took the ball and threw a wobbly pass downfield to O'Brien, who brought down the ball in his extended hands, juggled it and then regained possession at the ten-yard line. He rustled past two defenders, stumbled and dived into the end zone for the touchdown that gave Notre Dame a 12–6 lead.

When O'Brien got up, he saw Rockne beckoning and raced over to his coach. Rockne threw a blanket over O'Brien, then grabbed on to O'Brien's hand and shook it with considerable gusto and emotion.

As he watched the score, an injured Chevigny called out from the sidelines, "That's one for 'The Gipper' too."[5]

Army managed one final scare. And Notre Dame needed to call on all its emotional strength to hold on for the victory.

With less than two minutes remaining, Cagle returned the ensuing kickoff 55 yards, bringing the ball to the ten-yard line before collapsing because of exhaustion. He had to be carried off the field. Army's Richard Hutchinson then rushed for six yards to the four-yard line. He then carried again to the one.

But that's when the gun sounded. Army had come up one yard short. And Notre Dame had won one for "The Gipper."

Postscript: Notre Dame ended the season with losses of 27–7 to Carnegie Tech and 27–14 to USC, but the win over Army allowed Notre Dame to finish over .500 at 5-4. Army closed out its season with

University of Notre Dame halfback George Gipp. (Photo courtesy of Notre Dame's Sports Information Department.)

victories of 32–7 over Carleton and 13–3 over Nebraska before losing its finale to Stanford (New York City), 26–0. Army finished 8-2.

O'Brien never played another down of football after his winning touchdown catch, but "One-Play" O'Brien earned his niche in one of Notre Dame's greatest victories.

References

1. *Notre Dame 1990 Football Press Guide.*
2. Ibid.
3. Ibid.
4. Ibid.
5. Ibid.

Riegels Leads Cal
the Wrong Way

Georgia Tech 8, Cal 7 • *January 1, 1929*

Cal's Roy Riegels distinguished himself in the Rose Bowl against Georgia Tech with an inspired and ferocious display of blocking and tackling.

But, alas, Riegels' heroics were overshadowed and undermined by a single play.

In the second quarter of a scoreless game, Riegels made a huge miscalculation after recovering a fumble. His mistake? He ran the wrong way with the football. Georgia Tech turned that monumental gaffe into an 8-7 victory before 66,404 fans in Pasadena, California.

With about four minutes remaining in the first half, Georgia Tech halfback Stumpy Thomason scooted for a six-yard gain before being hit violently by Cal safety Benny Lom and end Irving Phillips. Thomason fumbled the ball forward and Riegels recovered at the Georgia Tech 34.

Without breaking stride, Riegels raced for the near sideline, but veered to his left to avoid four Georgia Tech players. After running away from would-be tacklers, Riegels moved into high gear — but in the wrong direction.

Lom, sensing the impending disaster, chased after Riegels in hot pursuit, but Riegels continued his sprint toward the wrong goal line. Lom finally caught up with Riegels at the three-yard line and grabbed hold of his teammate in an attempt to turn Riegels around. But by then it was too late. Riegels was swarmed on by a bevy of Georgia Tech players, who bounced Riegels and Lom into the end zone. The ball was ruled dead at Cal's one-yard line.

Trying to escape poor field position, Cal opted to punt on first down. But George Tech tackle Vance Maree blocked Lom's punt and the ball rolled out of the end zone for a safety. Georgia Tech was now ahead, 2–0.

Georgia Tech, which improved to 10-0, took an 8–0 lead when Thomason scooted 15 yards for a touchdown in the third quarter. The touchdown followed a 30-yard scamper by Warner Mizell.

Cal finally scored with 1:15 remaining in the game. Cal drove inexorably down the field and Lom climaxed the nine-play drive by throwing a 36-yard touchdown pass to Phillips. Stan Barr then kicked the extra point, leaving Cal only one point behind but serving to magnify Riegels' mistake.

Riegels, a center and middle linebacker, had attempted to atone for his error in the second half with a powerful performance that included a block and ensuing recovery of a Georgia Tech punt in the third quarter. Riegels recovered the blocked punt at the Georgia Tech 30, but Cal failed to capitalize.

Cal, finishing the season with a 6-2-2 record, showed a sizable advantage in first downs, 11–5, and in yards gained, 276–180.

But one ill-fated play turned the tide.

Riegels, a junior who had already been elected team captain for the following season, said in 1991 that he is asked about the infamous play all the time.

"I'll never forget it," Riegels said. "I didn't realize (my error) until Benny Lom chased me down the field and said I was going the wrong way. He grabbed my arm and started pulling me around."

Riegels added that his teammates treated him compassionately after the game.

"They were real quiet," Riegels said. "They didn't say anything derogatory or give me a bad time. I was just very embarrassed to

University of California center Roy Riegels. (Photo courtesy of California Sports Information Department.)

find out I had done it 'cause I had played a lot of football in my day."

Riegels' strange run was just one of many key plays in a game marked by numerous turnovers, big plays and breaks. One of the biggest breaks came on a play in which Lom picked up a fumble and raced 60 yards for an apparent touchdown in the second quarter. But referee Herb Dana ruled he had blown his whistle before the fumble.

Leading, 2–0, in the third quarter, Georgia Tech blocked another Lom punt, recovering at the Cal nine-yard line. But Georgia Tech was turned back after smashing into the line four times and ended up one foot shy of the goal line.

Lom emerged as probably Cal's most outstanding performer of the game, and he finished as the game's leading ballcarrier with 113 yards in addition to his excellent passing.

Cal's most memorable performance, however, was turned in by Riegels, the Golden Bears' 170-pound center who was the center of attention in this game.

16   Georgia Tech 8, Cal 7 (1929)

Postscript: Cal did not have the option of trying for two points and possibly tying the score after its late touchdown. College football rulesmakers did not allow for a two-point conversion try until the 1958 season.

Despite Georgia Tech's perfect record, USC (9-0-1) was named the national champion on the basis of the Dickinson ratings, a mathematical system that rated teams from 1924–40. The Associated Press' sportswriters and broadcasters poll did not start until the 1936 season.

Riegels' error resulted in his receiving one of football's most infamous nicknames: "Wrong Way" Riegels. Still, Riegels carved an undeniable niche as a talented football player. He was named to the All-Coast team after his junior season and was selected as an All-American after his senior season.

Later, he coached high school, junior college and armed forces football. "You know," Riegels said in 1990, "I really wasn't a bad football player. But for the life of me, I still don't know how or why I did what I did."[1]

Reference

1. *Sports Illustrated* (15 October 1990).

Columbia Sandbags Stanford
Columbia 7, Stanford 0 • January 1, 1934

Columbia reigned on Stanford's parade as Columbia recorded a surprising 7–0 victory in a Rose Bowl game played under intermittent showers in Pasadena, California.

Heavily favored Stanford piled up 272 yards in offense and 16 first downs, but Stanford failed to score despite repeated opportunities.

Columbia, by contrast, mustered only 114 yards and six first downs but scored the game's only touchdown when Al Barabas scampered 17 yards in the second quarter. From then on, Columbia protected its lead and protected it well, displaying a magnificent defense that clamped down whenever Stanford got close to scoring.

Columbia quarterback Cliff Montgomery. (Photo courtesy of Columbia University Department of Athletics.)

Not even vaunted running back Bobby Grayson could lead Stanford to a score although he finished with 160 rushing yards — more than the yardage accrued by all of Columbia's backs combined.

Was the rain a factor in the game?

Columbia quarterback Cliff Montgomery said in 1991 that it made all the difference in the world.

"Stanford hated it," Montgomery said. "They never played in rainy weather. We had a couple of bad rainy days during the fall, which included snow. If it had been a dry field, I don't think we would have won."

The adverse conditions affected both teams' passing attacks. "In those days, you didn't change the ball every time it got wet," Montgomery said. "The ball became heavy because it was saturated with water."

Stanford, which fell to 8-2-1, completed only 2 of its 12 passes for 23 yards. Montgomery hit only one of two passes, but his one completion led to the game's only touchdown. Right end Tony Matal made a diving catch of Montgomery's pass for a 23-yard gain and two plays later, Barabas scampered untouched around left end for the decisive score.

The game eventually evolved into a punting duel. Montgomery punted 14 times, averaging 37 yards, and often kicked on first and second downs. The hope was that Stanford would fumble the kick with a wet ball and Columbia would recover.

Fumbles played a big part in the game as two Stanford third-quarter drives expired with Grayson fumbles inside Columbia's 15-yard line.

"I remember on one play — it was fourth down and about two or three yards away from the goal line — that Grayson went into the line and in frustration fumbled intentionally into the end zone," Montgomery said. "He was hoping his team would recover, but [Columbia's Edward] Brominski fell on it and gave us a touchback."

Columbia, on the other hand, made good on its second-quarter scoring chance. Columbia's touchdown march started from the Stanford 45 after Montgomery returned a punt five yards. After Stanford was called for offsides, Matal caught Montgomery's 23-yard pass to bring the ball to Stanford's 17. Barabas then fumbled on the next play but recovered for a half-yard loss. The next play was one that Montgomery was waiting to spring on Stanford.

After faking to right halfback Brominski up the middle, he spun to his right and handed off to Barabas circling around to the left. Stanford's right end, Keith Topping, was trapped inside by a block from Brominski and Barabas found nothing but open spaces.

"When Barabas walked across the goal line," Montgomery said, "there was no one around him for twenty yards. They still don't know where he was."

Montgomery said that Ernie Nevers, Stanford's assistant coach, was aware of his spin move and the resulting reverse and had alerted Stanford Head Coach Tiny Thornhill about the possibility. "But Thornhill said the play would never work. He said the play was a joke," Montgomery recalled, "but it was the play that beat them."

After the touchdown, Columbia played conservatively thereafter, leaving the game in the hands of its defense. "We got more confidence as the game went on," Montgomery said. "We understood that Stanford didn't like the weather at all."

Columbia, which improved to 8-1, arrived in Los Angeles the day before the game amid a downpour. It was the heaviest 24-hour rainstorm in the history of the local United States Weather Bureau. The 24-hour total showed a whopping 7.31 inches of rain, bringing the storm's total rainfall to 8.27 inches.

"When we arrived in L.A., it had rained for three days," Montgomery said. "They had considered postponing the game for a day until the surrounding fire departments pumped over a million gallons of water out of the Rose Bowl. . . . And the Rose Bowl drained superbly well."

Stanford running back Robert (Bones) Hamilton said in 1991 that the wet conditions were a rude awakening for his team. Hamilton said Stanford got a peek at the Rose Bowl field the day before the game. "Three or four benches were completely off the ground floating around in water," he said.

Hamilton admitted his team was "disappointed and downcast" about the prospect of playing in the rain. But he said the team never lost hope during the game.

"Our team wasn't one to get discouraged," he said, "but we just couldn't overcome that slippery ball. Back where Columbia played, half their games were in the rain. But it was our first time in the rain. It was very disappointing to lose, but you have to give Columbia credit. Both teams played with the same ball, so you can't make excuses. They had more desire to win, I guess."

Postscript: Hamilton was a member of a large group of sophomores who played on Stanford's varsity for three years and became known as the "Vow Boys" for making two promises. Their first promise came after their freshmen team lost to USC in 1932. They vowed never again to lose to USC in their upcoming years on the Stanford varsity. And they never did. Stanford beat USC, 13-7, 16-0, and 3-0, the next three years. The Vow Boys made their second promise after losing to

Alabama, 29–13, in the 1935 Rose Bowl game. They vowed to reach the Rose Bowl game again the next year and vowed to win it — which they did, 7–0, over Southern Methodist.

Notre Dame Displays Luck of the Irish

Notre Dame 18, Ohio State 13 • November 2, 1935

Notre Dame's Bill Shakespeare helped write a surprise ending to the Fighting Irish's 18–13 victory over Ohio State in Columbus, Ohio.

Trailing, 13–0, at the end of three quarters, Notre Dame scored three touchdowns in the final period to defeat the nation's top-ranked team before 81,108 shell-shocked fans. And it was the unlikely Shakespeare who authored the winning touchdown pass after Notre Dame's brilliant halfback, Andy Pilney, was knocked out of the game late in the fourth quarter with the Buckeyes clinging to a 13–12 lead.

Pilney suffered torn cartilage in his knee after scrambling 32 yards to the Buckeye 19-yard line and was carried off the field on a stretcher.

In came Shakespeare to replace Pilney with half a minute remaining. Shakespeare's magnificent punting had kept Ohio State at bay throughout the game, but he was a much less dependable passer. Shakespeare was completing less than a third of his passes and had thrown a first-half interception that had launched Ohio State's second touchdown. Nonetheless, Shakespeare took right to the air. His first pass headed straight for Buckeye defender Dick Beltz, who had an interception and a Ohio State victory within his grasp.

But Beltz dropped the ball. And the Buckeyes would pay for the mistake.

Shakespeare faded back again, stopping at the Buckeye 38-yard line, before heaving a long pass downfield toward left end Wayne Millner. The Notre Dame receiver appeared well-covered as he raced into the end zone, but he made a sensational catch for the winning touchdown. It was the heavily favored Buckeyes' first loss after opening the season with five wins; Notre Dame improved to 6-0.

"I've thought a lot about the [touchdown] pass," said Shakespeare years afterward. "But I wake up nights dreaming about the one before it — the one the Ohio State guy had in his hands and dropped. If he'd held it, Wayne and I both would have been bums."[1]

Shakespeare delivered the coup de grace, but Pilney made it all possible with a spectacular exhibition of passing and zigzag running. Pilney set up Notre Dame's first touchdown early in the fourth quarter with a 26-yard punt return and his 12-yard pass to Francis Gaul that left Notre Dame at the Buckeye 2-yard line. From there, fullback Steve Miller crossed into the end zone to cut Ohio State's lead to 13-6.

The touchdown instilled some much-needed confidence in the Fighting Irish's offense, which responded with another determined drive minutes later. But Notre Dame's march was repelled when Ohio State recovered a Miller fumble in the Buckeye end zone.

Undaunted, Pilney engineered another drive when the Irish regained possession at their 20-yard line with three minutes remaining. Pilney caught a pass for 37 yards and threw a 33-yard touchdown pass to Mike Layden, the son of Notre Dame Coach Elmer Layden, to bring Notre Dame within 13-12. Wally Fromhart, however, missed the extra-point kick and Notre Dame remained a point behind.

Notre Dame then attempted an onside kick, but Ohio State was not surprised and recovered. Notre Dame demonstrated that it had the luck of the Irish because the Buckeyes — needing only to hold on to the ball to pull out the victory — fumbled it away. Pilney forced a fumble by Beltz and Notre Dame reserve Henry Pojman recovered at the Ohio State 49.

With the crowd in an uproar, Pilney dropped back to pass, dodged a strong rush and sprinted 32 yards before he was injured on a fierce tackle near the sideline.

"They put me on a stretcher and then carried me into the fieldhouse," said Pilney in 1991. "Then I heard the crowd and the trainer said to me, 'Andy, it's over. We won.' That's the last thing I remember because I got a shot and I went out."

Ohio State, as expected, dominated the first half behind a razzle-dazzle offense and an unyielding defense, which produced the game's first score. A pass by Layden in Ohio State territory was intercepted by

Frank Antennuci, who surrounded by tacklers, lateraled to Frank Boucher. Picking up a wave of blockers, Boucher raced 72 yards down the sideline for a touchdown.

The Buckeyes made it 13-0 early in the second quarter after Stan Pincura intercepted a Shakespeare pass with a shoestring catch. Joe Williams ran four yards for the touchdown and Ohio State seemed on the way to its expected rout.

But the second half belonged to Notre Dame. Pilney credited Notre Dame quarterback Fromhart with providing a lift at the start of the third quarter. "The first time we got the ball in the second half, Wally Fromhart jumped all over us in the middle of the field. He was kind of our leader both on and off the field," Pilney said.

"He said we looked like a poor football team despite the fact that we had a chance to win the national championship. He told us that unless we worked at it, we weren't going to do it. He told me that I'd have to throw the ball because they were using six- and seven-man lines.

"So in the second half, we passed more than we did the entire year. The big difference from the first half was that we just changed our strategy. Ohio State was looking for a lot of running and we passed the ball. We just befuddled them and broke the game open."

The Fighting Irish received additional inspiration from a halftime talk by Coach Layden, one of Notre Dame's famed Four Horsemen in the early 1920s. Layden concluded his pep talk by saying, "They won the first half. Not it's your turn. Go out and win this half for yourselves."[2]

The Fighting Irish's 18-0 second-half advantage was testimony that they did.

Postscript: The emotional victory did not generate the momentum that Notre Dame had hoped for. The Fighting Irish lost to Northwestern in their next game, 14-7, and then tied Army, 6-6, before concluding their season with a 20-13 victory over USC. Notre Dame finished 7-1-1.

References

1. *Notre Dame 1990 Football Press Guide.*
2. Ibid.

SMU's Wilson
Bests TCU's Baugh

Southern Methodist 20, Texas Christian 14
November 30, 1935

It was billed as the "Game of the First Half of the Century" in the Southwest Conference and the contest easily lived up to expectations.

An overflow crowd of 40,000 fans watched Southern Methodist and All-American halfback Bobby Wilson best Texas Christian and its All-American quarterback Sammy Baugh, 20–14, in Fort Worth, Texas.

But it was not easy.

SMU opened a 14–0 lead, but Baugh responded by guiding the Horned Frogs on a 74-yard scoring drive in the second quarter and passing eight yards to halfback Jimmy Lawrence for a touchdown early in the fourth quarter to tie the score at 14.

Then it was Wilson's turn for heroics.

The 147-pound Wilson produced the winning score on the Mustangs' next possession when he snared a 36-yard touchdown pass from Bob Finley on a fourth-and-seven play. The touchdown gave SMU a six-point lead, but TCU twice put a scare in the Mustangs late in the game when the Horned Frogs drove into scoring range.

SMU's victory was not assured until time ran out after Baugh connected with L. D. Meyer on a 17-yard pass that brought the ball to the SMU 35-yard line. Baugh, a junior, completed three consecutive passes on TCU's final drive and finished with nine completions for 116 yards in the final quarter alone.

It was a bitter defeat for TCU and a glorious victory for SMU. Both teams had entered the game 10-0 and with their sights on the Rose Bowl and a national championship.

Wilson, a senior, scored two touchdowns, his first coming on a nine-yard run around end early in the second quarter to boost SMU into a 14–0 lead. His second touchdown capped a 53-yard drive that appeared to have bogged down at the TCU 36. But from there, Finley lofted a long pass that Wilson snared with a diving catch at the four-yard line and his momentum carried him into the end zone.

SMU halfback Bobby Wilson. (Photo courtesy of SMU's Sports Information Department.)

"I looked over my shoulder one way and the ball was thrown over my other shoulder," said Wilson in 1991. "I turned fast and caught it on the other side. It wasn't a sensational catch. It was a routine job."

It was routine for Bobby Wilson, considered the best back in the country that year.

Wilson said the fourth-and-seven play was a pass all the way and there was no fake involved.

"Finley went back into deep punt formation," Wilson said. "It wasn't much of a fake. He put it in the air as far as he could. He must have dropped to about the fifty. The pass wasn't a thing of beauty, but it was there."

Baugh, who was playing defensive back on the play but was not guarding Wilson, said TCU was not expecting a punt.

"We knew what they were going to do," said Baugh in 1991. "The rule then was that if you pass in the end zone on fourth down, it's just like a punt if it's incomplete. You bring it to the twenty. When you'd get to about the other team's forty, you'd go ahead and throw the ball in the end zone. It's just like a damn punt if it's not complete."

Later in the quarter, Baugh led TCU to the SMU 28-yard line, but the drive stopped there when Baugh's fourth-down pass was knocked down. Baugh, who had many of his passes dropped, started slowly, but caught fire in the fourth quarter and finished with 16 completions in 41 attempts for 184 yards.

TCU's final drive started after Wilson lost a fumble at the TCU 26-yard line.

"I had no business fumbling the ball," said Wilson. "I was on the sidelines and I was sure the ball was going out of bounds, but it went the other way. It really scared us when they started to move the ball right after."

It was a rare Wilson mistake. He finished with 97 yards in 14 carries.

"He was one of the great runners in the Southwest Conference," Baugh said. "The Southwest didn't get much publicity except in our area. But he was a great runner and a fine football player."

Wilson returned the compliments about Baugh.

"He was the only man I ever saw who could throw the soft pass and the hard pass," Wilson said. "He had control of the ball whenever he threw."

TCU did win in one area: statistics. The Horned Frogs had an edge in yardage (362–315) and first downs (25–17).

"If we had played them every day, we'd probably win half of them," Baugh said. "We were both good football teams."

Postscript: SMU (12-1) was named the national champion in Madison Bell's first year as SMU head coach although the Mustangs dropped a 7–0 decision to Stanford in the Rose Bowl.

TCU won its final two games, beating Santa Clara, 10-6, and LSU, 3-2, in a rainy Sugar Bowl, to end the season 12-1. Baugh highlighted the Sugar Bowl with the longest run of the game, a 44-yard scamper. Baugh passed for 1,322 yards and 19 touchdowns his junior season and led TCU to a 9-2-2 season and a 16–6 victory over Marquette in the first Cotton Bowl as a senior. Baugh was named an All-American his final two seasons at TCU and finished fourth in the first Heisman Trophy vote in his senior season.

Wilson's touchdown reception against TCU may have been the biggest single play in SMU history. The score led to SMU's appearance in the Rose Bowl and paid off the mortgage on the new SMU stadium. SMU owed $85,000 on its stadium and the money was due. Mustang Athletic Director James H. Stewart had borrowed the money from a bank to pay off the note. The Rose Bowl game brought in $85,000 in revenue to the SMU coffers and, as a result, Wilson's scoring reception became known as the "$85,000 Touchdown."

Wilson was the first Southwest Conference back to win All-American recognition, earning the honor in 1934 and 1935. He led the conference in scoring both as a junior (48 points) and a senior (72 points). He played a year of professional football in 1936 for the Brooklyn Dodgers.

Baugh Enjoys Stirring TCU Farewell

Texas Christian 16, Marquette 6 • January 1, 1937

Although Arkansas won the 1936 Southwest Conference championship, another Southwest Conference member, Texas Christian University, got the invitation to the first Cotton Bowl.

There was a simple and logical explanation for selecting TCU.

The Horned Frogs possessed Sammy Baugh, the two-time All-American quarterback who would be playing his final game as a collegian after a magnificent three-year career.

And he did not disappoint the 17,000 fans in Dallas who watched him put on another show.

Showcasing his talents as a passer, kicker, runner and tackler, the 6-foot-2, 180-pound Baugh led TCU to a 16–6 victory over Marquette. The game pitted two of the finest backs in the country in Baugh and Marquette's Ray Buivid. Baugh completed 5 of 13 passes for 110 yards and one touchdown with two interceptions, rushed for 28 yards in two carries, returned three punts for 49 yards and averaged 36 yards in three punts. Buivid, meanwhile, completed 10 of 19 for 130 yards with three interceptions.

The difference was Baugh led TCU to 16 points, while Marquette's only score came when Art Guepe returned Baugh's punt 60 yards for a touchdown.

Baugh said generously that the player of the game had to be TCU senior end L. D. Meyer, who scored all of TCU's points. Meyer, the 168-pound nephew of TCU Coach Dutch Meyer, caught two touchdown passes and kicked a field goal and an extra point.

Texas Christian quarterback Sammy Baugh. (Photo courtesy of TCU Sports Information Office.)

28   Texas Christian 16, Marquette 6 (1937)

"L. D. Meyer was a substitute," said Baugh in 1991. "We had two ends that were better than him."

Meyer's first touchdown late in the first quarter put Texas Christian ahead for good. He combined with Baugh on a 30-yard touchdown pass to boost the Horned Frogs into a 10–6 lead. Meyer was shoved into the end zone by Buivid, who caught him at the two-yard line. Meyer also scored on an 18-yard reception in the second quarter, outjumping two defenders on a halfback pass from Vic Montgomery, who had faked a reverse.

Meyer, filling in for the hospitalized Willie Walls, hit a field goal from the 23-yard line early in the first quarter to give TCU a 3–0 lead. The field goal was set up by Baugh's 23-yard pass to Scott McCall.

The player of the game might have been Meyer but the man of the hour was Slingin' Sammy Baugh. With Baugh sitting on the bench in the final minutes, the fans roared for him to return to the game. The exhortations worked as Baugh returned amid a thunderous ovation.

It was a fitting tribute to the player who passed for 853 yards and 11 touchdowns his sophomore year, 1,322 yards and 19 touchdowns his junior year and 1,296 yards and 11 touchdowns his senior year. Baugh also had distinguished himself as a spectacular punter and stalwart defensive player. Playing safety, Baugh intercepted 56 passes in his career.

Baugh had expected a stiff test from Marquette. Not only did Marquette boast Buivid, but it had a breakaway threat in Guepe, who Baugh called "the best running back I had seen at that time."

Furthermore, Baugh conceded his own team was far from imposing.

"We had a fair team, but not one that I would consider a real strong team," said Baugh, adding that TCU was stronger during his 12-1-1 junior season. "I felt we could represent the Cotton Bowl fairly well, but we didn't have the team that two years down the road [behind quarterback Davey O'Brien] would win the whole darn thing." (TCU finished No. 1 in the country for the 1938 season.)

Still, TCU lived up to its ranking as the 16th team in the country, improving to 9-2-2. Meanwhile, 20th-ranked Marquette fell to 7-2.

TCU dominated not only on the scoreboard, but in the statistics. TCU registered 16 first downs to Marquette's 10. And TCU generated 323 yards; Marquette had only 185.

Postscript: In the first balloting for the Heisman Trophy, Baugh finished fourth with 39 points. Yale end Larry Kelly was first with 219 points, Nebraska fullback Sam Francis was second with 47 and Buivid was third with 43.

TCU Coach Meyer said Baugh was "the greatest athlete I ever saw."[1] Baugh was a first-round draft choice of the Boston (Washington) Redskins in 1937 and was more responsible than any other player for the National Football League's passing evolution. Baugh played 16 seasons for the Redskins, completing 1,693 of 2,995 passes for 21,886 yards and 186 touchdowns.

Twice Baugh passed for six touchdowns in the pros. When he retired in 1952, Baugh held NFL career records for most passes, completions and touchdown passes. He also led the NFL in punting four times, including the 1940 season in which he averaged a whopping 51.0 yards a kick.

Baugh, a three-time All-Pro, led the Redskins to five divisional titles and two championships. Baugh threw three long touchdown passes in the 1937 NFL championship game to key the Redskins' 28–21 victory over the Chicago Bears.

Baugh coached the New York Titans from 1960–61 and the Houston Oilers in 1964. He was named to the College and Professional Football Halls of Fame.

Reference

1. *Texas Christian 1990 Football Press Guide.*

USC Subs Sink Duke
USC 7, Duke 3 • January 2, 1939

USC junior quarterback Doyle Nave played only 28½ minutes during the regular season, but his time finally came during the Rose Bowl in Pasadena, California.

Trailing, 3–0, against Duke, the Trojans mounted a last-minute drive. Quarterback Grenny Lansdell led USC from the Trojans' 39 to Duke's 34 in six plays as the clock wound down to about two minutes.

At that time, USC Coach Howard Jones approached Nave, a fourth-string quarterback.

"Doyle, I'm thinking of putting you in," Jones said.

"What have you got in mind?" Nave asked.

"The 27 series," Jones replied. "Get the ball to [Al] Krueger. He's the best end we have for getting open."[1]

Nave did just that.

After USC was penalized five yards for excessive time-outs, Nave connected with Krueger for a 13-yard gain. It was second and two at the Duke 26.

On the next play, Nave hit Krueger for a nine-yard gain. It was first and 10 at the Duke 17.

Nave then hit Krueger again, but it went for a two-yard loss. It was second and 12 at the Duke 19.

Once again, Nave faded back and focused on Krueger, although the sophomore end was being guarded by standout Eric Tipton, whose booming punts had kept the Trojans bottled up for most of the game. Dropping back deep, Nave fired diagonally across the field to Krueger.

"I faded back to the 31- or 32-yard line," Nave said in 1988, "and, as soon as Al made his move, I threw that damn thing as hard as I could right into the corner, and he was there."[2]

The 19-yard touchdown pass to Krueger with 40 seconds remaining gave USC a dramatic 7-3 victory before 89,452 fans, and its fifth Rose Bowl victory without a loss.

That the seventh-ranked Trojans could score at all against third-ranked Duke represented a breakthrough. Entering the game, Duke had fashioned a 9-0 record and had not been scored upon.

USC (9-2) had threatened to score in the fourth quarter when the Trojans recovered a fumbled punt by Duke's Bob Spanger on the Duke ten. Three plays later, USC remained on the ten. A field-goal try by Phil Gaspar to tie the score sailed wide and Duke appeared headed for another shutout.

Duke, however, failed to sustain a drive after taking possession and punted to the Trojans' 39-yard line where Lansdell signaled for a fair catch.

Two minutes later, Nave entered the game sporting a bandage over a cut on his forehead — an injury he sustained in a scrimmage. Nave had played in only four previous games during the season. He had scored a touchdown against Washington State, run 68 yards for a touchdown

Al Krueger's game-winning catch from Doyle Nave. (Photo courtesy of USC Sports Information Department.)

32   USC 7, Duke 3 (1939)

against Oregon, gotten in for one play against Stanford and played less than two minutes against UCLA.

Krueger said in 1991 that he did not second-guess the decision to remove Lansdell for Nave.

"I just wanted to win the game," Krueger said. "That was the only thing on my mind."

Krueger, who split time at end with Bill Fisk, played the second and fourth quarters. Krueger said that was part of his coach's strategy in which Jones would alternate 11-man teams each quarter.

"They put Fisk and the heavy team in first to wear the opposition down," Krueger said, "and then let the light ones score the touchdowns."

Duke and USC failed to cross the other's 35-yard line until Tipton connected on a 24-yard pass to George McAfee late in the third quarter.

The completion set up Duke on the Trojan 25. On fourth and one, Tony Ruffa kicked a field goal from the 23 to give Duke a 3-0 fourth-quarter lead.

But three points would not stand up.

Postscript: The strange circumstances about Nave's sudden entry were revealed years after the game.

Joe Wilensky, a USC assistant coach, had been an admirer of the Nave-to-Krueger combination in practice and was convinced that the pair could pull out the victory.

During the game, Wilensky was operating a phone from the bench, relaying messages from assistant coaches in the press box.

Wilensky told Assistant Coach Nick Pappas on the sideline that Assistant Sam Barry, supposedly in the press box, wanted Nave to come off the bench in those crucial final minutes.

After Krueger scored, Pappas noticed that Barry was not in the press box, but on the sideline. Wilensky was forced to admit to Pappas that he had faked taking a call from Barry. Pappas did not tell anyone about the hoax for ten years and only revealed that story after the death of Jones.

After playing his senior season at USC, Nave was drafted in the first round by the Detroit Lions but decided against playing pro football. He died in 1990 at 75.

Krueger caught a touchdown pass from quarterback Ambrose Shindler in USC's 14-0 over Tennessee in the 1940 Rose Bowl. He played two seasons for the Washington Redskins from 1940-42 and one (1946) with the L.A. Dons.

"I'd say Doyle Nave was as good as [the Redskins' six-time All-Pro] Sammy Baugh," Krueger said. "I wouldn't say Doyle was better and I wouldn't say Sammy Baugh was better. I played with both and I caught touchdowns from both."

References

1. *Los Angeles Times*, 11 December 1990.
2. Ibid.

Harmon's Birthday Party Produces Michigan Celebration
Michigan 41, Cal 0 • September 28, 1940

Michigan's Tom Harmon got his senior season off to a fast start against Cal before 54,000 fans at Memorial Stadium in Berkeley.

On his 21st birthday, Harmon scored four touchdowns, passed for another and even avoided an attempted tackle by a drunken spectator darting out from the stands. Michigan won the season opener, 41-0, on a day Harmon looked every bit as unstoppable as the great Red Grange of Illinois.

Harmon ran 94 yards for a touchdown on the opening kickoff. His second touchdown came when he retrieved a punt that had gone over his head and dashed 70 yards.

The Michigan halfback's third touchdown produced a surreal scene. Harmon, getting the ball on an end sweep, took off from his 14 and sprinted down the sideline. As he neared the goal line, a bald-headed spectator ran onto the field and dived for Harmon's leg, grabbing it but failing to pull him down and prevent the 86-yard touchdown run. Police later came onto the field to take away the spectator, Bud Brennan, a local realtor.

Harmon added a seven-yard touchdown run to go along with four extra-point kicks, giving him 28 of Michigan's 41 points. He also threw a touchdown pass to Dave Nelson.

But Harmon's chance meeting with a rabid Cal fan drew the most attention. Harmon's teammate, All-American tackle Al Wistert, had a clear view of the confrontation. "Harmon was running for another touchdown and I'm moving up the field with him, but there's nobody left to block," Wistert said in 1991.

Wistert continued, "Now I see this guy coming out to try to tackle him from the stands. I say, 'Look out Tom.' He spots the guy, sidesteps him and the guy falls down.

"Afterward, I found out the guy was talking to his friend in the end zone. They were two Cal alums. Harmon was having a big day. After he scored his second touchdown, this guy turns to his friend and they're drinking pretty good, 'My Gosh, if that team can't stop Harmon, I'm going to tackle him myself.'

"About that time, the friend says, 'Hey, if you're going to tackle him, you better get out there, because here he comes again.'"

After the game, Harmon said, "It was most embarrassing. Think how I would have felt after slipping past 11 well-conditioned athletes to be downed by a woozy alum."[1]

As if another odd twist to the story were needed, Brennan visited the Michigan dressing room after the game. He and Harmon became unlikely friends over the years, playing golf and talking frequently as they crossed paths. Harmon never pressed charges.

As memorable as the game was for Michigan and Harmon, equally unforgettable was the Wolverines' trip to Berkeley. Michigan became the first intercollegiate team to make a trip by airplane. The school chartered three United Airlines' DC-3s and transported its party of 53 across the country, stopping in Des Moines, Denver and Salt Lake City before arriving in San Francisco.

"It was a real thrill to be making my first plane ride, and that was true of a lot of the guys," Wistert said. "And then to be flying out to California. We got very sick looking out the window. They circled the field of the Ann Arbor area a few times to let us look around, and that made us more airsick."

Along the way, players were invited up to the front cabin to visit with the pilot. "I got sick as a dog and the reason why was I was all eyes," Wistert said.

Wistert said Harmon was a one-of-a-kind athlete who was a remarkable competitor. "In practice, he didn't punt that outstandingly," Wistert said, "but put him in a game under competition and that son of a gun would be punting like the best punter in the country."

Michigan halfback Tom Harmon. (Photo courtesy of Michigan Historical Collections, the Bentley Historical Library, University of Michigan.)

Harmon earned 14 varsity letters in high school in Gary, Indiana, so his athletic ability was already legendary when he arrived at Michigan. But for those who got close to him, Harmon's talents still were surprising.

"Tom Harmon was a fantastic athlete," Wistert said. "He was very fast. He was a natural runner who used his blockers well."

Michigan Coach Fritz Crisler called Harmon "the greatest player I've ever coached."[2]

Postscript: Harmon, nicknamed "Gary Ghost" and "Old 98," was the runaway winner of the Heisman Trophy in 1940. Michigan finished 7-1, losing only to Minnesota, 7–6. Minnesota went on to win the national championship while Michigan was ranked third by the Associated Press.

From 1938–40, Harmon rushed for 2,134 yards, passed for 1,396 yards and scored 237 points with 33 touchdowns. He was on the cover of *Time* and *Life* and even starred in a movie about himself, *Harmon of Michigan*, in 1941. He was selected first in the 1941 National Football League draft but played in the rival American Football League with the New York Americans.

He served in the U.S. Air Force during World War II and was awarded a Silver Star and Purple Heart. Harmon survived bailouts from two destroyed planes in enemy territory. He played for the Los Angeles Rams in 1946 and 1947, but injuries from the war prevented him from being his old self. He eventually pursued a career in broadcasting.

After the war, Harmon married Hollywood film actress Elyse Knox. Among his children was Mark Harmon, later a quarterback for UCLA and actor. Tom Harmon was elected to the College Football Hall of Fame. He died in 1990 at 70 of a heart attack soon after completing a round of golf at Bel-Air Country Club in Los Angeles.

Wistert was one of three brothers who played left tackle at Michigan, and each one made All-American. Wistert became an All-Pro with the Philadelphia Eagles.

References

1. The Associated Press, 29 September 1940.
2. Ibid.

New Formation Fits Stanford to a T

Stanford 21, Nebraska 13 • January 1, 1941

How successful was Stanford's season with its revolutionary T-formation?

Give Stanford a perfect 10.

Stanford, the first college team to use the T-formation as its basic offense, finished 10-0 after polishing off Nebraska, 21–13, before 90,000 fans in the Rose Bowl in Pasadena, California.

The previous year, Stanford was a lowly 1-7-1 under Coach Tiny Thornhill, but Stanford attained a reversal of fortune after Clark Shaughnessy took over the helm and inserted the T-formation into his team's offense.

Shaughnessy found the right players to run his offense, which featured junior quarterback Frankie Albert directly behind the center and men in motion. The athleticism and trickery of Stanford's backfield

Stanford halfback Hugh Gallarneau.

were evident against the befuddled Cornhuskers. Albert, halfbacks Hugh Gallarneau and Pete Kmetovic and fullback Norm Standlee rushed for 277 yards to confound Nebraska — just like they had confounded their previous nine opponents. For good measure, Albert added a touchdown pass, an 85-yard quick kick and three extra-point kicks.

"We were a ball-control team," said Albert in 1991, "and we just concentrated on grinding out the yards on the ground."

Afterward, Nebraska Coach Biff Jones conceded to reporters that Albert and Co. was just too tough. "Go tell Clark Shaughnessy I'll buy him 120 acres of fine corn land if he'll tell me where we can get a Frankie Albert. That kid's got too much pass, too much kick, too much noodle for us. What a job he did out there."[1]

Nebraska, however, was far from a pushover against Stanford. The Cornhuskers, in fact, pushed over the game's first touchdown, needing only seven plays to score on their first possession. Fullback Vike Francis' two-yard run gave Nebraska a 7–0 lead.

Shaughnessy said Stanford remained calm despite the quick score. "It did look bad," said Shaughnessy afterward, "but I can't say I was particularly worried. These boys of mine have a way of getting their touchdowns and I figured they'd get started."[2]

Albert agreed that Stanford was unfazed by Nebraska's early touchdown. "That didn't bother us too much," he said. "They scored in

Stanford Coach Clark Shaughnessy. (Photo courtesy of Stanford Sports Information Department.)

five, six minutes so that still left us with about 50 minutes to play. Unless we rolled over and played dead, we had a chance to show what we could do. And it allowed us to recognize that Nebraska had a fine offense."

Late in the first quarter, Stanford tied the score on Gallarneau's 11-yard touchdown run. But Nebraska went ahead again in the second quarter. After a Kmetovic fumble, Nebraska's Herman Rohrig threw a 33-yard touchdown pass to Allen Zikmund to push the Cornhuskers into a 13-7 lead.

But Stanford was not one to get discouraged — not the "Wow Boys" — descendants of Stanford's "Vow Boys" of the 1930s.

Stanford, known for its tremendous running game, also had a nifty left-handed passer in Albert. And he combined with Gallarneau on one of the two most spectacular plays of the game to give Stanford the lead

Stanford 21, Nebraska 13 (1941)   39

again. Albert launched a high, hard pass that the stretching Gallarneau hauled in at the 10-yard line and sped into the end zone for a 40-yard touchdown.

Albert's extra-point kick gave Stanford a 14–13 lead and Stanford would not trail again.

Kmetovic gave Stanford some breathing room in the third quarter with an electrifying 39-yard punt return for a touchdown. After catching the punt, Kmetovic wheeled to the left, then wheeled to the right where he picked up blocking. Stanford blockers cut down every Nebraska would-be tackler in sight, including the 200-pound Francis, who somersaulted off a block and was injured.

The punt return was the coup de grace for Stanford.

Nebraska, whose record slipped to 8-2, would not threaten thereafter, finishing with zero points for the second half. The Cornhuskers could take solace in the fact that they put on a valiant goal-line stand in the third quarter, holding Stanford on downs from eight inches away.

It was a feat rarely done against Stanford during the team's glorious season.

Postscript: Stanford finished second in the Associated Press' final poll that was taken before the bowl games. Minnesota was No. 1 at 8-0. Nebraska was seventh. For the season, Stanford outscored the opposition, 196–85, but Albert said the team was not sold on the T-formation from the outset. "We scrimmaged the freshmen before the season started and they beat us. They pushed us all over the field," Albert said. "They didn't have trouble finding the football and I'm sure the coaches felt the same way we did — very disappointed." But Stanford routed San Francisco, 27–0, in its season opener and things began to fall into place.

Albert finished fourth in the Heisman Trophy voting with 90 points and placed third the following season with 336 points as a senior when Stanford was 6-3 in Shaughnessy's final year as Stanford coach.

"Shaughnessy was great," Albert said. "He was very serious about football and very dedicated and so well-respected. He would diagram a play on the board and say, 'Norm Standlee is going to score five touchdowns on a fullback counter play,' and we would just poke one another because we hadn't even scored five touchdowns the whole (previous) season. But he gave us a lot of confidence. He got an A for coaching and we got a B for running the plays."

Shaughnessy, a star fullback at the University of Minnesota, also made his mark in the professional ranks. As an unofficial consultant to the Chicago Bears, Shaughnessy helped spruce up the Bears' attack in 1940 when they went on to win the NFL championship with a 73–0 victory over the Washington Redskins.

Four years later, Shaughnessy served as an adviser to the Redskins and helped quarterback Sammy Baugh learn the T-formation. Shaughnessy became the Los Angeles Rams' head coach in 1948 and guided the team to the 1949 Western Conference title. In 1949, Shaughnessy introduced the "three-end offense" as a regular part of the offense. He died in 1970 at 78.

Albert was the first player signed by the San Francisco 49ers of the new All-America Football Conference, playing as a T-formation quarterback for seven seasons. He also played a season for the Calgary Stampeders in the Canadian Football League.

In 1941 Coach Frank Leahy introduced the T-formation at Notre Dame and his success enabled him to win four national titles. Army's Earl Blaik went to the T-formation and produced national championships in 1944 and 1945, compiling a 25-game winning streak and a 32-game unbeaten streak.

References

1. *Los Angeles Times*, 2 January 1941.
2. Ibid.

Texas' Layne Lights Up the Scoreboard
Texas 40, Missouri 27 • January 1, 1946

Texas quarterback Bobby Layne, the leader of the Longhorns, capped his sophomore season with a breathtaking performance in which he scored four touchdowns and passed for two others to lead Texas to a wild-and-woolly 40–27 victory over Missouri before 46,000 fans in the Cotton Bowl.

Layne also kicked all four of his team's extra points, thus having a hand in every Longhorn score.

Missouri, showcasing its newly instituted T-formation, was a worthy opponent despite being a decided underdog. The Tigers matched Texas touchdown for touchdown for most of the game. But Missouri could not quite keep up with Bobby Layne.

The Longhorns' fiery leader finally put the game out of reach with a 15-yard, fourth-quarter touchdown run after a pitchout from fullback Ralph Ellsworth. The score gave Texas a 40–21 lead and some breathing room at last. Ellsworth said Layne's touchdown sprint came on a broken play.

"It was an improvised play. I was going off right tackle — we were running from a single wing — and the ball was snapped to me," said Ellsworth in 1991.

"The hole was closed and Bobby was just standing there so I pitched it to him and he went in for the score. He scored every possible way and figured in every score. As they say, he did everything but sell tickets."

Layne's two touchdown passes measured 48 and 15 yards and both were caught by Bill Baumgardner. In all, Texas passers completed 13 of 14 for 264 yards. Layne caught a touchdown pass himself, hauling in a 49-yard pass from Ellsworth in the fourth quarter that gave the Longhorns a 34–21 lead.

Layne's passes were not always pretty, but they typically were effective, reaching his receiver whenever he was open.

"I can't say he was a pure passer because his spirals weren't tight. He was a finesse passer — his passes were easy to catch," said Ellsworth, who led Texas' ground game with 82 yards.

The Southwest Conference champion Longhorns opened the scoring in the first quarter on Layne's 48-yard pass to Baumgardner. But the Tigers tied the score later in the quarter on a 65-yard touchdown pass from Bill Dellastatious to Roland Oakes.

And thus a pattern was set.

The tenth-ranked Longhorns (10-1) would keep scoring but so would Missouri. "It was a fun game from a spectator's standpoint," Ellsworth said. "It would have been fun to watch all the scoring. Whoever had the ball scored. We couldn't stop their T-formation and they couldn't stop Bobby Layne."

Layne scored from one yard out late in the first quarter to give the Longhorns a 14–7 lead and scored again from one yard late in the second quarter to break another tie and boost the Longhorns into a 21–14 lead. This time, the unranked Tigers would not catch up.

Texas All-American end Hub Bechtol said that he never thought

Texas quarterback Bobby Layne. (Photo courtesy of Texas Sports Information Department.)

his team was in danger of losing. "We were never concerned we were going to get beat — at least I wasn't," said Bechtol in 1991.

One of the biggest reasons for Texas' confidence was the presence of Bobby Layne. With Layne at the controls, Texas staged touchdown drives of 75, 60, 69, 74, 80 and 60 yards and totaled 19 first downs. But Missouri (6-4) also moved the ball easily, racking up 22 first downs.

"We were very confident," said Missouri's massive 6-foot-2½, 270-

pound tackle Jim Kekeris in 1991. "If we could have stopped Bobby Layne and if we could have defensed Bechtol, we could have beaten them. They were able to complete their passes, but they couldn't run through us — we ran through them."

Missouri halfback Bob Hopkins rushed for 125 yards and a touchdown and teammate Leonard Brown gained 121 yards. The Tigers were primed for an upset, but the Texas quarterback had other ideas.

"He was unreal, just unreal," said Kekeris about Layne. "His record showed what he did in the pros. He was an outstanding, magnificent ballplayer."

"Bobby had tremendous desire," added Ellsworth. "He was a great leader and he became more so as he progressed in the pros. He was never beaten, he just ran out of time. That's how I always thought of him."

Postscript: Layne led Texas to an 8-2 record the following season and a 10-1 record in 1947 when the Longhorns were ranked fifth. Layne was eighth in the Heisman Trophy voting in 1946 and sixth in 1947. He ran for 305 yards and passed for 1,115 in 1946 and passed for 1,145 yards in 1947.

Layne enjoyed a brilliant career in the National Football League, beginning in 1948 when he played for the Chicago Bears. His greatest success came as a member of the Detroit Lions (1950–58).

The 6-foot-2, 190-pound Layne led the Lions to the 1952 and 1953 NFL championships. He threw for 26,769 yards and 196 touchdowns and rushed for 2,451 more in the NFL. He also scored 372 points on 25 touchdowns, 120 extra-point kicks and 34 field goals.

More than his statistics, Layne was remembered for his competitiveness that propelled his teams to decisive touchdowns in the final minutes.

"He demanded only the best and would accept only the best," SMU's Heisman Trophy winner Doak Walker said. "Here is a man who was a general on the field and off the field in every way. He was the greatest two-minute quarterback I have ever seen."[1]

Layne was selected to both the College and Professional Football Halls of Fame. He died in 1986 at 59.

Reference

1. *Los Angeles Times,* 2 December 1986.

Army, Notre Dame
Battle to a Draw

Army 0, Notre Dame 0 • November 9, 1946

An offensive showdown between the two top-ranked teams in the country turned into a defensive standstill as No. 1 Army and No. 2 Notre Dame played to a 0–0 tie before 74,000 fans at New York City's Yankee Stadium.

It was a shocking outcome considering that two of the nation's most prolific offenses failed to produce a single point.

Army had entered the game 7-0 behind its 30-points-a-game offense fueled by its touchdown twins of fullback Doc Blanchard (Mr. Inside) and halfback Glenn Davis (Mr. Outside). And Notre Dame had racked up a 5-0 record with a 35-points-a-game average behind its sensational junior quarterback Johnny Lujack.

Both teams had their share of scoring opportunities. Army moved into Notre Dame territory ten times. And the Fighting Irish crossed midfield four times and registered the biggest threat of the game in the second quarter when they staged an 85-yard march. Sparked by the running of Gerry Cowhig and Bill Gompers and the passing of Lujack, Notre Dame reached Army's four-yard line. But on a fourth-and-two play from there, Gompers got hauled down on a run around right end one yard short of a first down.

The Irish found themselves within scoring range again in the third quarter when Notre Dame's John Mastrangelo recovered a fumble at the Army 34. But Cadet quarterback-defensive back Arnold Tucker snuffed out the threat with an interception, one of his three interceptions for the day.

Tucker's interception seemed to give Army momentum. On the next play, Blanchard raced around end, cut toward the sideline and sped toward the end zone. Only Lujack had a shot at Blanchard. With the crowd screaming and on its feet, Lujack dived for Blanchard's ankles and upended him at the Irish 37, saving the touchdown.

"They said Blanchard couldn't be stopped one on one in the open field, yet I did it," said Lujack afterward. "I really can't understand all the fuss. I simply pinned him against the sideline and dropped him with a routine tackle."[1]

University of Notre Dame quarterback Johnny Lujack. (Photo courtesy of Notre Dame Sports Information Department.)

46   Army 0, Notre Dame 0 (1946)

Davis, however, said that the tackle was far from routine.

"It was a lucky deal," said Davis in 1991. "As Blanchard passed him, Lujack dived and three fingers hit him and crossed him."

Still, it was a 26-yard gain by Blanchard and Army appeared to be inexorably rolling toward a touchdown. But minutes later, Terry Brennan, Notre Dame's leading ballcarrier with 69 yards in 14 carries, blunted the drive by intercepting Davis' pass at the Irish eight-yard line.

Blanchard, a senior, finished as Army's leading ballcarrier with 50 yards in 18 carries. Davis, a senior, ran for 30 yards in 17 carries and completed two of six passes for 30 yards.

Both coaches expressed disappointment with the outcome.

"I suppose I should be elated over the tie," said Notre Dame's Frank Leahy afterward. "After all, we didn't lose, but I'm not."[2]

Army Coach Earl "Red" Blaik expressed similar sentiments.

"There is no jubilation in this dressing room," Blaik said. "It was a vigorously fought, terrific defensive game. Both teams played beautifully on the defense and that affected both teams' attack."[3]

Davis said he believed both coaches played more conservatively than usual because of the closeness of the game.

"I think if the game was played over, both coaches would certainly play it differently," Davis said. "Both coaches went to three yards and a cloud of dust and didn't really open up. I think if either team would have scored early, it would have been good for the game and changed the way the game was played.

"It was so conservatively played that I believe on the last play of the game, I was put out on the right and Blanchard quick-kicked. The theory was that if there was any kind of a bobble, I could pick it up and go on for the score."

Army, the national champion in 1944 and 1945, had its 25-game winning streak ended by a Notre Dame team that had suffered humiliating defeats of 59–0 and 48–0 at the hands of the Cadets the two previous years.

Notre Dame had not forgotten those overwhelming losses. The week before the game, the Irish took breaks from practice to chant, "Fifty-nine and forty-eight, this is the year we retaliate."

Notre Dame students got into the act too. They sent daily postcards to Blaik and signed them "SPATNC" (Society for the Prevention of Army's Third National Championship).

Notre Dame Coach Frank W. Leahy. (Photo courtesy of Notre Dame Sports Information Department.)

But neither team demonstrated superiority on the field. Notre Dame had ten first downs to Army's nine. The Cadets gained 224 yards, the Irish 219.

The fourth quarter demonstrated clearly that the only winner was the defense. The Irish mustered only one first down in the fourth quarter — the same total as Army.

Postscript: Army went on to crush Penn, 34–7, before closing out its season with a surprisingly difficult 21–18 victory over a relatively weak Navy team that thoroughly outplayed the Cadets in the second half. Still, the Cadets finished undefeated for the third consecutive season at 9-0-1. In a three-year period from 1944–46, Army's teams compiled a brilliant record of 27-0-1. Army, however, was ranked No. 2 to Notre Dame in the final Associated Press poll. The Irish closed out their season in impressive style. Notre Dame trounced Northwestern, 27–0; Tulane, 41–0; and USC, 26–6, to finish at 8-0-1 and No. 1 in the country.

It was Leahy's first season back with the Irish after serving in the Navy during World War II and marked his second national championship team. His teams would win four national titles in his 11 seasons as Notre Dame coach.

Davis won the Heisman Trophy with 792 points after finishing second in the voting the previous two years. Lujack picked up 379 points to finish third and Blanchard was fourth with 267 points and Tucker fifth with 257. Blanchard had won the Heisman Trophy in 1945.

Lujack won the Heisman Trophy the following season when Notre Dame repeated as the national champion. En route to a 10-0 season in 1947, Notre Dame defeated Army, 27–7.

References

1. *Notre Dame 1990 Football Press Guide.*
2. Ibid.
3. Ibid.

Army Weathers Stormy Second Half to Outlast Navy

Army 21, Navy 18 • November 30, 1946

It appeared to be a total mismatch. Army was the No. 1–ranked team in the country, undefeated in three seasons. Navy had lost its previous six games.

Army was the two-time defending national champion and boasted three-time All-American running backs Glenn Davis (Mr. Outside) and Doc Blanchard (Mr. Inside). The Cadets were favored by a whopping 28 points in the regular-season finale.

It was a mismatch on paper. But it was no mismatch on the field as Army barely held on for a 21–18 victory before 102,000 fans at

Navy running back Pete Williams.

Philadelphia's Municipal Stadium to remain undefeated for the third consecutive season. Navy ended the season at 1-8-1 but could take solace in its gallant, though losing, battle.

The Cadets (9-0-1) lived up to their lofty billing in the first half, rolling to a 21–6 halftime lead. But in the second half, Navy turned around the game with a relentless ball-control offense that featured

Navy running back Bill Hawkins.

fresh backs from its armada of reserves. Navy quarterback Reaves Baysinger and running backs Pete Williams, Lynn Chewning, Al McCully, Bill Hawkins and Bill Earl kept hammering away at an Army team that could not match Navy's multitude of reserves.

Navy scored the only two touchdowns of the second half to pull within three points early in the fourth quarter. After forcing Army to punt late in the fourth quarter, Navy began a thrilling last-minute drive from its 33-yard line. A 17-yard pass from Williams to reserve end Phil Ryan and a 20-yard fourth-down run by Chewning helped bring the ball to the 3-yard line with only 1:30 remaining.

Navy was knocking on the door of one of the biggest upsets in college football history.

At the Army three-yard line, fullback Chewning got the call on first down but was stopped at the line of scrimmage by Goble Bryant and Hank Foldbert. It was now second down.

Again Chewning got the call, but again he was stopped at the line of scrimmage. It was now third down, the ball still resting at the three-yard line.

But before Navy could get off the next snap, the Midshipmen were called for a delay-of-game penalty, and the ball was brought back to the eight-yard line. Still third down.

Navy shifted from the T-formation to a single-wing formation and Hawkins got the snap. He took two steps toward the line before lateraling to Williams, who was upended at the five-yard line. A Navy substitute rushed on the field to call time-out but was too late as the gun sounded.

It was a moral victory for Navy, but not one that was altogether satisfying.

"We were proud of what we had done," said Williams in 1991, "but we didn't celebrate because we truly felt we could have won the ballgame and should have won the ballgame. Of course, if we had won, we would have celebrated in grand style."

Williams added that Navy's record was misleading. Five of their losses came against teams that finished the season ranked within the top 13. And the Midshipmen were blown out only against Notre Dame (28–0).

"I think our ballclub was not as bad as people thought we were," Williams said. "If you review our season, we really had given a good accounting of ourselves, with the possible exception of the Notre Dame game and we had given a good accounting of ourselves in the first half of that game. We were a pretty decent team."

Davis said that it was vital that his team stop Navy from fulfilling its upset mission.

"We were so close to getting beat," said Davis in 1991. "If we would have lost that game, in the annals of sports history, we would have been just another football team. We were so much better than they were. It just proves that if a team lets down and another starts rolling, you better watch out."

Navy's final goal-line series brought out Davis' leadership qualities.

"I'll never forget it," Davis said. "I was going back to the huddle, and said, 'For crying out loud, we're going to lose everything we accomplished unless we hold these guys.'"

And hold Army did.

Davis admitted that Army probably took Navy lightly after the Cadets scored three touchdowns in the first half to take a 15-point halftime lead. Army built its advantage on touchdown runs of 46 and 26 yards by Blanchard and 13 yards by Davis.

"We were up, 21–6, in the first half and thought we were going to make it 42–6," Davis said. "We just bogged down in the second half and Navy had the ball all the time."

Navy scored its two second-half touchdowns on drives of 78 and 35 yards. Hawkins scored from two yards out in the third quarter to reduce Army's lead to 21–12. On the second play of the fourth quarter, Earl threw a three-yard scoring pass to Leon Bramlett that left Navy behind, 21–18.

In the end, the difference was the extra-point kicks. Army's Jack Ray converted all three of his, while Navy's Bob Van Summern and Hawkins failed to convert their three attempts.

Among the crowd was President Truman, who watched the first half on the Navy side when Army dominated the game. In the second half, Truman shifted to Army's side. But that was Navy's half to dominate, except for the last few plays.

Postscript: The sluggish performance against Navy did not help Army in the national rankings. Army dropped to No. 2 in the final Associated Press poll behind Notre Dame, which won its last three games in resounding fashion. Army had won the national championship the previous two seasons.

Army completed its three years with Davis and Blanchard as its star running backs with a 27-0-1 record. Army was 9-0 in both 1944 and 1945 and 9-0-1 in 1946.

"Our 1946 team was not nearly as good as either of our other teams," said Davis, the Heisman Trophy winner in 1946. "The 1946 team didn't have nearly the reserves as the other ones. Blanchard was hurt most of the season and [quarterback Arnold] Tucker dislocated his shoulder and was hurt a lot. Our best team was the 1945 one."

Davis scored 51 touchdowns — 20 coming in 1944 — to total 306 points at Army. Blanchard scored 231 points in his career, including 19 touchdowns during his Heisman Trophy–winning year in 1945.

Columbia Rallies to Snap Army's 32-Game Unbeaten Streak

Columbia 21, Army 20 • October 25, 1947

Unheralded Columbia shattered Army's aura of invincibility before 35,000 fans at the Lions' Baker Field in New York City. And Columbia did it with a second-half flourish that was as impressive as it was unexpected.

Columbia, entering the game with a 2-2 record, rallied from a 20–7 half-time deficit to surprise Army, 21–20, and break the Cadets' 32-game unbeaten streak. The Cadets suffered their first loss since they dropped a 13–0 decision to Navy in their 1943 season finale.

Included in that four-year streak in which Army won 30 games and tied two was the Cadets' 48–14 pummeling of Columbia in 1946.

"We thought we could play with them in 1946," said Columbia quarterback Gene Rossides in 1991, "because we had a terrific team. But we didn't jell until 1947."

Rossides expected that the Lions would be more competitive in the rematch, partly because he did not believe that Army would be quite as potent as the Cadets' 1946 edition, which finished second in the national rankings. Gone were halfback Glenn Davis (Mr. Outside), fullback Doc Blanchard (Mr. Inside) and talented quarterback Arnold Tucker, all of whom had graduated.

Their replacements, quarterback Arnold Galiffa and running backs Bill Gustafson and Rip Rowan, were a formidable group but were not in the same class as their predecessors, who won Heisman Trophies both in 1945 (Blanchard) and 1946 (Davis) and led Army to national championships in 1944 and 1945.

Still, Army (3-1-1) appeared in control after a dominating first half. The Cadets moved the ball at will, shut down Columbia's running game and limited the Lions' offense to a handful of spectacular catches by left end Bill Swiacki. Late in the second quarter, Rowan rambled 84 yards for a touchdown, his second of the half, to stake Army to its 13-point halftime lead. Although Jack Mackmull missed the extra point, it hardly seemed to matter. But that vital point would come back to haunt the Cadets.

Instead of deflating the Lions, however, Rowan's touchdown turned out to act as a catalyst for Columbia's second-half show of strength. The Lions used Rowan's score as a means of motivating themselves.

"That touchdown run really got us mad," Rossides said. "We weren't down when we went into the clubhouse at halftime, just mad. We thought we could stop their running and their passing wasn't as dangerous without Tucker. And we knew we could score."

Columbia had scored its first touchdown in the second quarter on a six-yard run by Lou Kusserow after Army had taken a 14-0 lead. It was a notable touchdown because it was the first points Army had allowed during the season. In its previous four games, Army had outscored its opponents, 100-0. Kusserow's touchdown destroyed any Columbia notion that Army was invincible.

And after a scoreless third quarter in which Columbia's quarterbacks completed nine passes, the Lions took command in the final period. With Rossides showing an accurate passing touch and rendering Army helpless on pass defense, Columbia closed to within 20-14 early in the fourth quarter. Swiacki made an acrobatic catch in the end zone on a 53-yard pass from Rossides. It was one of nine receptions for Swiacki, four of which were of the spectacular variety.

"Swiacki's great catch in the end zone was a broken play, but one we had worked on," Rossides said.

"It was a down-and-out on the sideline. Bill was covered and I didn't have time to find a second receiver because [Army's] Joe Steffy was in on me. Bill was covered in front, so he went up and I threw over the safety and Bill made a diving catch in the end zone. You could feel a surge in our team after that."

Midway through the final quarter, Columbia scored its final touchdown. Coach Lou Little's Lions required only 1:27 to march 66 yards in six plays. Ventan Yablonski ran 11 yards off tackle to move Columbia to the Lions' 45.

Then Rossides gained 22 yards on a sneak to bring the ball to the Army 33. After Kusserow gained four yards, Rossides hit Swiacki on a 26-yard pass to give Columbia first and goal at the Army three.

Rossides gained a yard on first down, then Kusserow ran two yards for the touchdown that tied the score. Yablonski kicked the all-important winning extra point, his third of the game.

Army tried to rally, as Galiffa hit Rowan with a 30-yard pass. But the play was called back because of an offside penalty. Galiffa completed an eight-yard pass to John Trent, but his next pass was intercepted by Kusserow near midfield.

Columbia then clinched the victory by staging a ball-hogging drive deep inside Army territory to run out the clock, whereupon Swiacki was hoisted on the shoulders of several of his teammates and carried off the field.

"People don't realize that there was 6½ minutes to play when we got our winning score," said Rossides, who completed 18 passes.

"It wasn't that Columbia got a lucky break and won on the last play of the game. We killed the clock at the end. I just want to make the point that we beat them. We didn't get lucky."

Postscript: Army finished its season 5-2-2 and ranked 11th in the nation by the Associated Press. Steffy won the Outland Trophy for being the nation's best interior lineman. Columbia did not lose another game during the season, finishing 7-2 and ranked 20th.

Swiacki signed with the New York Giants in 1948 and played with them for three seasons before being traded to the Detroit Lions.

He later became an assistant coach with the Giants and the Los Angeles Rams and served as head coach of the Canadian Football League's Toronto Argonauts from 1955–56. He died in 1976 at 53.

Rice's Moegle Magnificent Despite Off-the-Bench Tackle

Rice 28, Alabama 6 • January 1, 1954

Rice halfback Dicky Moegle enjoyed an extraordinary game and took part in an extraordinary play in Rice's 28–6 victory over Alabama in the Cotton Bowl in Dallas before 75,504 fans.

Moegle dashed for three touchdowns on runs of 79, 95 and 34 yards. He set a collegiate bowl record by averaging 24.1 yards a carry en route to rushing for 265 yards in only 11 carries. His second touchdown was particularly noteworthy because it was one for the books — the rule books.

With two minutes left in the first half and Rice holding a 7–6 lead, Moegle ran a sweep to the right side from his team's five-yard line. Moegle sprinted into the clear on the sideline, pulling away from Alabama's defenders.

Then Alabama senior Tommy Lewis got into the act to make for one of the wackiest plays in college football history. Lewis, who was watching the action from the sideline, bolted from his bench as an unsuspecting Moegle drew near.

When Lewis darted toward Moegle, the Rice junior speedster veered slightly away to avoid a direct hit. But Moegle could not avoid Lewis, who brought him to the ground at the Alabama 38-yard line.

Referee Cliff Shaw instantly awarded Moegle a 95-yard touchdown. Shaw cited a rule that awards a touchdown if "anyone other than a player or official . . . tackles a runner who is in the clear and on his way to a reasonably assured touchdown."[1]

Moegle said in 1991 that he was knocked unconscious by the blow. He lay on the field for about a minute as Rice trainer Eddie Wojecki attended to him.

Recounting the play, Moegle said that after he raced into the clear on the sideline, he looked over his shoulder to see if any Alabama defenders were in hot pursuit.

"All of a sudden, I see this guy leaning down," Moegle said. "He was in some crouch. I thought he had dropped his head gear, but I didn't see any head gear. Then it dawned on me that this guy had come off the bench.

"He didn't tackle me down. He blocked me down. He got square in front of me and then I veered a step to the left. He still hit me a good lick. He could have broken my back or seriously injured me if I hadn't veered. When you cut or veer, it takes a lot of the impetus off the block.

"As it was, he still knocked me out."

At halftime, Lewis apologized to Moegle and Rice Coach Jess Neely. A remorseful Lewis explained his actions afterward by saying "I'm too emotional. I guess I'm just too full of Alabama. He just ran too close."[2]

"I didn't know what I was doing," Lewis added. "When I had him tackled, I jumped and got back on the bench. I kept telling myself, 'I didn't do it. I didn't do it.' But I knew I did."[3]

Lewis said in 1991 that he was standing next to halfback Corky Tharp when Moegle sprinted in his direction. "I turned my head away from the play," Lewis said, "and I told Tharp, 'He's going to go all the way.' When I looked back on the field, he was in my face. I could have reached out and grabbed him. I just waylaid him. I've had to answer for it and live with it for the rest of my life.

"Recently, I was talking to Bart Starr, who was the quarterback and defensive safety for our team that game. He was playing both ways and he told me that if he hadn't missed a tackle on the play, all the heartache and headaches never would have happened.

"I'm still embarrassed by it, but my friends, especially my closest friends, never mention it. They know how I feel about it. I ended my college career on a sour note. But I thought the press handled it badly. They made me out to be a lowly substitute, while actually I was the starting fullback and the alternate captain."

Lewis led 13th-ranked Alabama, the Southeastern Conference champion, to the first score of the game. After Starr intercepted his first of two passes to give Alabama possession at the Rice 49, Alabama moved briskly to a touchdown and a surprising 6-0 lead. Lewis smashed over from the one-yard line for the touchdown.

Moegle, however, took over from that point. Rice needed Moegle's heroics because its All-American fullback, David (Kosse) Johnson, reinjured his ankle in the first quarter and was lost for the game.

Early in the second quarter, Moegle sprang into action, slashing inside right tackle and cutting away from defenders en route to a 79-yard touchdown. Leroy Fenstemaker's conversion gave Rice a 7-6 lead and the Southwest Conference co-champion Owls would not be headed.

Alabama (6-3-3) replied with a 54-yard run by halfback Bill

Oliver, but the drive ended at the Rice five-yard line when Starr fumbled. On the next play, Moegle slipped through a gap on the right side and raced untouched for 53 yards before Lewis left his bench and upended him. Moegle got credit for a 95-yard touchdown and the sixth-ranked Owls (9-2) opened a 14-6 lead.

Even after being stunned by Lewis' tackle, Moegle wasn't through. He capped his amazing day with a 34-yard touchdown run in the third quarter to climax a 67-yard drive.

Looking back at the Lewis incident 37 years later, Moegle said the play never really disturbed him. "The only thing I regret, if I have a regret, is that the off-the-bench tackle overshadowed my All-American season the following year," Moegle said.

"I had a better year as a senior than I had as a junior. I was the leader in the conference in scoring, the leader in the conference in rushing and the leader in the conference in yards per carry. . . .

"But I guess it's better to be remembered for something than for nothing."

Postscript: Moegle enjoyed an All-American season the following year, leading Rice to a 7-3 record and a 19th national ranking by the Associated Press. He finished sixth in the Heisman Trophy balloting. In his career, he averaged 6.6 yards, carrying 267 times for 1,773 yards.

Moegle, who changed his name to Maegle in 1962 because it was being mispronounced so often, was drafted in the first round by the San Francisco 49ers and was named All-Pro as a defensive back in 1957. He played seven years in pro football, finishing as a player-coach under the Dallas Cowboys' Tom Landry.

Lewis played two years of professional football with the Ottawa Rough Riders, leading the Canadian Football League team in rushing and scoring both years. He also coached high school football for three years in Florida and Alabama. After his career at Alabama, Starr led the Green Bay Packers to five National Football League championships and two Super Bowl victories.

References

1. Brown, Gene. *The New York Times Scrapbook Encyclopedia of Sports History — The Complete Book of Football.* (Indianapolis/New York: Bobbs-Merrill Company, Inc., 1980).
2. *Los Angeles Times,* 2 January 1954.
3. Ibid.

Kaiser's First Field
Goal Lifts Michigan State

Michigan State 17, UCLA 14 • January 2, 1956

Michigan State's David Kaiser got his first chance to become a hero in the Rose Bowl and he took advantage of the opportunity.

Kaiser was a third-year sophomore transfer from Notre Dame who started at end on both offense and defense. Since the seventh grade, he also had a fondness for kicking. He'd practice punting and kicking whenever possible.

He had never made a field goal in college, but Michigan State Coach Duffy Daugherty turned to Kaiser against UCLA when the game was on the line.

Michigan State and UCLA were tied at 14 in the closing seconds. Regular kicker Gerald Planutis had missed two field goals earlier in the game.

Daugherty sent out Kaiser to attempt a 41-yard field goal. There were 100,890 fans on their feet. Kaiser had no time to think of the pressure. He had just resumed kicking after being sidelined with an injury.

"When I kicked the ball, it was a floater," he said in 1991. "I kicked it a little high. It was heading right for the uprights and I said, 'My God, it's going to be good.' I turned around because I wanted to see the referee throw up his arms. Then the whole team hit me."

There was so much confusion after the field goal that the public address announcer said that Planutis had made the winning kick.

Kaiser's field goal with seven seconds left gave Michigan State a 17–14 victory in a game that might have been the most exciting contest of the season.

The kick was preceded by a delay-of-game penalty on Michigan State after the Spartans had thrown a kicking tee onto the field.

The Spartans had a chance to break the 14–14 deadlock with 1:34 left, but Planutis missed a 40-yard field goal, giving UCLA the ball on its 20.

Then the Bruins began to self-destruct. Quarterback Ronnie Knox didn't know whether to run out the clock or try for the win by passing.

UCLA line coach Jim Myers gave him a hand signal from the

sideline to pass. Although the rules prohibited signaling plays from the bench, officials rarely called the penalty.

But this time, the officials handed out a 15-yard unsportsmanlike penalty, putting the ball on UCLA's five.

"I must say it was an exceptional call," said UCLA Coach Red Sanders afterward.[1]

On the next play, Knox went back to pass, retreating into the end zone before throwing an incompleted pass. Penalty flags flew again.

At first, Knox was called for intentionally grounding, which would have given Michigan State a safety. But the officials ruled the Bruins had an illegal receiver downfield. The ball was moved to UCLA's one-yard line.

Knox, acting on his own, decided he needed to get the ball out of there fast if the Bruins wanted to maintain a tie. He punted to the UCLA 40 despite it being only second down.

The Bruins were called for its third consecutive penalty when guard Hardiman Cureton hit Michigan State's Clarence Peaks moments before he caught the punt. A 15-yard interference penalty put the ball on UCLA's 19.

Victory was within reach for the Spartans. On Michigan State's first play, there was a fumble, with the Spartans recovering. The officials also called a penalty on the Spartans for pushing, and the ball was moved back to the 30.

A run and pass moved the ball to the 19. Time was running out when the Spartans suddenly threw the football tee onto the field with 15 seconds left. They called time-out almost at the same time the tee was thrown.

Some felt the throwing of the tee was a signal to call time-out and violated the same coaching rules that had cost UCLA 15 yards earlier.

But no unsportsmanlike penalty was called. Michigan State, however, was cited for a delay-of-game penalty, leaving Kaiser with a 41-yard kick, which he converted for the winning score.

Kaiser had tried two field goals earlier in the season but missed both. That season, field goals were not popular.

"If you had fourth down and three yards to go, you went for the touchdown," Kaiser said. "That was the philosophy in the 1950s."

But Kaiser loved to kick. He was the last person to leave practice so that he could work on his kicking.

Michigan State 17, UCLA 14 (1956)   61

Michigan State kicker David Kaiser. (Photo courtesy of Michigan State Sports Information Department.)

62   Michigan State 17, UCLA 14 (1956)

Kaiser was told so suddenly about being selected to attempt his last-second kick that he had no time to consider the pressure.

"After years and years of practice, my conscious mind didn't kick, but my subconscious took over because I had practiced so long," he said.

The game started badly for Michigan State. On the Spartans' first offensive play, All-American quarterback Earl Morrall's pass was intercepted by Jim Decker, who was tackled at the Spartan 16. Fullback Bob Davenport scored on a two-yard run and UCLA led, 7–0.

The score was 7–7 at halftime after Morrall threw a 13-yard touchdown pass to Peaks. Michigan State went up, 14–7, early in the fourth quarter on a 67-yard halfback pass from Peaks to end John Lewis.

Knox, who was not expected to play much for UCLA because of a leg injury, rallied the Bruins. A 47-yard pass to Decker set up Doug Peters' one-yard touchdown run to tie the score, 14–14.

Soon it was Kaiser's chance to earn a place in the hearts of Michigan State fans.

Postscript: The victory left Michigan State with a 9-1 record and the Associated Press No. 2 national ranking behind unbeaten Oklahoma. UCLA (9-4) was ranked fourth.

Morrall completed only 4 of 15 passes for 38 yards in the Rose Bowl but finished fourth in the Heisman Trophy balloting. He ended up playing 21 years in the National Football League for six teams. Morrall won the NFL passing title in 1968 while serving as a replacement for injured Baltimore Colts quarterback John Unitas. He was selected the NFL player of the year and led the Colts to Super Bowl III. In 1972, Morrall won the American Football Conference passing title in helping the Miami Dolphins to a 17-0 record. He passed for 20,809 yards and 161 touchdowns in the NFL.

Kaiser had a brief tryout with the Cleveland Browns before retiring to become a businessman in Michigan. He said in 1991 that he is constantly reminded of his heroics.

"Here's something that happened thirty-five years ago," Kaiser said, "and since that time, two weeks won't go by without someone asking, 'By the way, aren't you the guy who kicked the field goal?'" He kicked only one other field goal in his collegiate career, in an all-star game in Miami. "It has given me a certain amount of notoriety," Kaiser said.

Sanders died before the 1958 season. He had a career record at

Michigan State quarterback Earl Morrall.

64   Michigan State 17, UCLA 14 (1956)

Vanderbilt and UCLA of 102-41-3, including a 9-0 mark and the United Press International national championship as UCLA coach in 1954.

Reference

1. *Los Angeles Times*, 3 January 1956.

Syracuse's Brown Scores NCAA-Record 43 Points

Syracuse 61, Colgate 7 • November 17, 1956

When it comes to truly magnificent individual performances, few can top the record-breaking day enjoyed by Syracuse running back Jim Brown.

Before a Syracuse crowd of 39,701 fans, Brown accounted for an NCAA-record 43 points with six touchdowns and seven conversion kicks in the Orangemen's 61–7 victory over Colgate.

If ever a running back looked like an All-American, Brown fit the description. He rushed for 197 yards in 22 carries and scored touchdowns on runs of 1, 15, 50, 8, 19 and 1 yard.

Brown, 6-foot-2 and 228 pounds, ran over and around the helpless Colgate defenders. By halftime, when Syracuse held a 27–7 lead and Brown had scored all 27 points, the press box announcer proclaimed, "The score is now Brown 27, Colgate 7."

Brown started the scoring with a one-yard run to cap Syracuse's opening 75-yard drive. On the Orangemen's next possession, he went 15 yards for a touchdown and added the conversion kick, giving Syracuse (7-1) a 14–0 lead.

After Colgate (4-4) scored on a ten-yard touchdown pass, Brown unleashed his most spectacular touchdown of the day, taking a pitchout and racing 50 yards down the right sideline for a touchdown. Brown missed the extra point, making the first-quarter score 20–7. Brown added an eight-yard touchdown run for a 27–7 halftime lead.

In the third quarter, someone other than Brown finally scored for

Syracuse running back Jim Brown. (Photo courtesy of Syracuse Sports Information Department.)

66 Syracuse 61, Colgate 7 (1956)

Syracuse. Quarterback Chuck Zimmerman plunged over from the one. Then Brown scored on a 19-yard run for a 41-7 Syracuse advantage. Brown's sixth touchdown came in the fourth quarter on a one-yard run to make the score 55-7.

Thirty-five years later, Brown said, "I don't have too many comments on any games. It was a record. I remember that. It made a difference in my career at Syracuse."

Brown rarely talked about his exploits, preferring to let his actions speak for themselves. But then Syracuse Assistant Coach Roy Simmons, Sr., talked glowingly in 1991 about Brown's performance.

"He was sensational," Simmons said. "He was good anytime, but that day he had a hot game. He ran as fast as he had to to get the job done. He'd rather run over a guy than run around them. They couldn't do anything."

Colgate defensive end Kevin Conwick said in 1991 that trying to tackle Brown was a miserable experience.

"It was absolutely hair-raising," Conwick said. "He was absolutely the most phenomenal, physical creature who has ever existed. We could tell from their formations where Jim lined up if he was going left or right. If he lined up deep, he was going to the right. If he lined up tighter, he'd probably come off tackle on my side.

"From scouting, we could tell with ninety percent confidence which way he was going. We slanted to that side, but it made no difference."

The game became so frustrating for Colgate that end Al Jamison, 6-foot-4 and 220 pounds, struck Brown with an elbow after a conversion kick, forcing Brown to briefly leave the game. Brown knew who had hit him and got his revenge later in the game.

"Jamison went downfield and they left him wide open," Conwick said. "Jimmy was playing defensive back. Jamison caught the ball in the clear. Jimmy came up with about a ten-yard run and just picked this huge creature up and dropped him on his shoulder.

"His shoulder separated about three inches. It was the worst separation I've ever seen. It was total retaliation. You don't mess with Jim Brown. Al Jamison was not a dumb man, but he made a dumb mistake."

Overall, Syracuse rushed for 511 yards. The 43 points Brown scored alone equalled the most points previously scored by a Syracuse team.

"He did it all — breaking tackles and knocking people down," Simmons said. "He could do anything."

"We couldn't wait for him to go into the pros," Conwick said. "'Wait until Jim has to play guys all his size.' It made no difference. It was so pleasing to see Jim's rookie year in the NFL. In leading the league in rushing, nobody else could tackle him either. It was absolute vindication."

Brown was tough, physical and enjoyed playing all sports. He also threw the discus and played lacrosse. Simmons was Brown's lacrosse and boxing coach at Syracuse. One time, Brown had a boxing match against a teammate who weighed 225 pounds.

"I had to stop the bout because Jim was so vicious," Simmons said. "He could have been champion. He could hit so hard."

In a North-South all-star lacrosse match at Johns Hopkins University in Baltimore, Brown scored five goals.

"They allowed blacks to sit anywhere in the stands that game," said Conwick, who played on the same team with Brown in that all-star game. "I think it was the first time at Johns Hopkins Stadium that blacks sat on an integrated basis. Before the game, the team got together, coach gave his talk, we're about to break up and Jim Brown says, 'One moment. I'd like to say something. This is the first time my people have been able to sit in a stadium wherever they want. That means a lot to me and I hope you all help me play a great game.'

"You never would have guessed he had that sensitivity. Then he went out and played a great game."

Postscript: From 1954–56, Brown rushed for 2,091 yards, scored 25 touchdowns and accumulated 187 points for Syracuse. He ended his Syracuse career by rushing for 132 yards and scoring 21 points in a 28–27 loss to Texas Christian in the Cotton Bowl.

Syracuse finished the season 7-2 and ranked No. 8 by the Associated Press. Brown finished fifth in the Heisman Trophy voting, which was won by Notre Dame quarterback Paul Hornung. Brown was a first-round pick of the Cleveland Browns, for whom he became one of the greatest backs in National Football League history.

Brown was the NFL rookie of the year and later the NFL most valuable player in 1958 and 1965. He led the league in rushing for eight consecutive seasons, finishing with an NFL-record 12,312 career yards and 106 rushing touchdowns. He gained 100 or more yards in 58 games during his NFL career. In 1963, he set an NFL single-season rushing record with 1,863 yards. Brown retired at the end of the 1966 season at 30, having never missed a game in nine seasons.

After retiring, he became an actor and businessman.

Notre Dame Shatters Oklahoma's 47-Game Winning Streak

Notre Dame 7, Oklahoma 0 • November 16, 1957

It was vindication for Notre Dame Coach Terry Brennan.

With their fourth-year coach under fire, the Fighting Irish turned in a rousing effort to shatter heavily favored Oklahoma's 47-game winning streak — college football's all-time record — with a stunning 7–0 victory before 63,170 fans in Norman, Oklahoma.

Halfback Dick Lynch's three-yard touchdown run on fourth down late in the fourth quarter broke a scoreless tie and allowed Notre Dame to break a two-game losing streak.

For Brennan, it was a sweet victory. Brennan's Fighting Irish had lost to Oklahoma, 40–0, in South Bend, Indiana, the previous year — a season in which they registered their first losing record in 24 years with a 2-8 mark. Furthermore, the Fighting Irish had just dropped back-to-back games to Navy and Michigan State in one-sided fashion before heading for Norman and almost certain defeat against the nation's second-ranked Sooners, who had won their first seven games of the season.

But Notre Dame (5-2) pulled out of its tailspin behind a rock-ribbed defense that stopped the two-time defending national champion Sooners' run-oriented offense cold and an offense that mustered an 80-yard touchdown drive in the closing minutes.

Nick Pietrosante, a powerful 210-pound fullback, was the workhorse on Notre Dame's winning drive, smashing consistently up the middle for sizable gains as the Fighting Irish rolled to a first and goal at Oklahoma's eight-yard line. From there, Pietrosante chewed up four yards up the middle to bring the ball to the four. On second down,

Notre Dame Coach Terry Brennan. (Photo courtesy of Notre Dame Sports Information Department.)

Lynch was stopped for no gain. Quarterback Bob Williams then carried up the middle for one yard, leaving the Irish facing fourth and three with 3:50 remaining.

Disdaining the field goal, Notre Dame scored the game's only touchdown as Lynch carried three yards around right end, dashing into the end zone standing up.

Brennan said in 1991 that he bypassed a field-goal attempt on fourth down for several reasons. He said he feared kicker Monty Stickles might be hampered by a bad angle with the ball so close to the goal line. And Brennan also expressed confidence that his fourth-down call would work.

"We just wanted to do the sure thing," Brennan said.

And the sure thing in this case was for Williams to fake inside to Pietrosante before pitching the ball to Lynch around right end.

"When you're down at the goal line, and every one of the defenders is in the gaps," said Brennan, "where do you go? Outside."

"They were in tight, real tight, just waiting for me to give the ball to Pietrosante," Williams said. "Well, I just faked to him and tossed out to Lynch and it worked like a charm."[1]

Oklahoma, an 18-point favorite, had shown a propensity during its winning streak for scoring the decisive touchdown in the fourth quarter and this late-game magic become a trademark of Oklahoma Coach Bud Wilkinson's teams. But this time, Oklahoma's desperate attempt to catch up was blunted by an interception. The crowd then rose and saluted the gutty Notre Dame team with a thunderous ovation.

Pietrosante finished as Notre Dame's leading ballcarrier with 56 yards in 17 carries and Lynch gained 54 yards in 17 carries.

Oklahoma, which had been averaging 300 yards a game, was held to 98 yards on the ground and 47 in the air. Clendon Thomas was Oklahoma's leading ballcarrier with 36 yards in 10 tries.

"Oklahoma was a fine football team," Brennan said. "And Bud Wilkinson was a fine football coach. But he was predictable and we felt if we could stop their four or five basic plays, we had a chance to win. And we did."

One of Oklahoma's biggest weapons was the punting by Thomas and David Baker, who kept Notre Dame bottled up near its end zone in the third quarter. But the Sooners could not capitalize.

"I was willing to settle for a scoreless tie in the third quarter," said Wilkinson afterward. "I felt at the start of the second half we had a good chance. But after we couldn't get going, even with our tremendous punting to their goal, I was ready to settle for a scoreless tie."[2]

Oklahoma's best scoring threat came in the first quarter when the Sooners drove to Notre Dame's 13-yard line before they were held on downs. "They were just better than we were today," Wilkinson said. "They deserved to win."[3]

Notre Dame not only stopped Oklahoma's winning streak, but the

Irish broke the Sooners' national record of scoring in 123 consecutive games. Interestingly, Notre Dame was the last team to defeat Oklahoma, defeating the Sooners, 28–21, at the start of the 1953 season. Oklahoma was tied, 7–7, by Pittsburgh in its next game before beginning its amazing streak.

Postscript: The loss to Notre Dame was Oklahoma's only defeat during a 10-1 season in which the Sooners finished as the fourth-ranked team. Oklahoma trounced Duke, 48–21, in the Orange Bowl. Notre Dame finished the season unranked with a 7-3 record.

Brennan, a former three-year starting running back at Notre Dame, often called the streak-stopping victory over Oklahoma "the greatest thrill of my athletic career."[4] Brennan coached the Fighting Irish for five seasons, compiling a 32-18 record. Pietrosante distinguished himself as a stellar running back for the Detroit Lions.

References

1. *Notre Dame 1990 Football Press Guide.*
2. Ibid.
3. *Los Angeles Times,* 17 November 1957.
4. *Notre Dame 1990 Football Press Guide.*

Cannon Provides Firepower for LSU

Louisiana State 7, Mississippi 3 • October 31, 1959

With one fantastic punt return, Louisiana State's Billy Cannon forever endeared himself in the hearts of Louisiana's legion of football fanatics.

The clash between top-ranked LSU and third-ranked Mississippi attracted 67,000 fans to LSU's Tiger Stadium. And when the game had ended and LSU had triumphed, 7–3, for its 19th consecutive victory, all anyone wanted to remember was Cannon's 89-yard punt return early in the fourth quarter for the game's only touchdown.

"That," said LSU Coach Paul Dietzel afterward, "was the greatest run I ever saw in football."[1]

Louisiana State running back Billy Cannon. (Photo courtesy of LSU Sports Information Department.)

Cannon retrieved a punt by Mississippi's Jack Gibbs with his team down, 3–0, and thousands of local folks pleading for the legendary Billy Cannon to make something happen.

Gibbs' punt was a good one, traveling 47 yards to the 11-yard line. Dietzel had a rule against fielding punts inside the 15, but the ball easily bounced into Cannon's hands and he began his dash for the end zone. He was hit almost immediately but kept churning his powerful legs. He was hit again and looked ready to go down. He was hit one more time but continued forward, unwilling to hit the turf.

Then Cannon broke free near the LSU 40-yard line and bolted to the end zone.

"Cannon ran down the sideline and I could have reached out and touched him," Mississippi defensive back Billy Brewer recalled 32 years later.

Brewer was standing on the sideline as Cannon raced toward

history. "Had I been in there, I would have made the tackle," insisted Brewer, who certainly did his best to disrupt Cannon and LSU, recovering three fumbles.

Even after Cannon's touchdown gave LSU a 7–3 lead with ten minutes left, Mississippi didn't fold. The Rebels (6-1) drove the length of the field, setting up an all-important goal-line stand. On fourth and goal from the two, Mississippi's Doug Elmore was stopped by LSU's Bo Strange and Warren Rabb. With 18 seconds left, LSU (7-0) took possession and ran out the clock. It was the seventh consecutive game in which LSU had not allowed a touchdown.

Except for Cannon's punt return and a 22-yard field goal by Mississippi's Robert Khayat, neither team could score. It was a defensive slugfest, in which field position meant everything.

Brewer, later to become head football coach at Mississippi, marveled at the defensive strategy.

"We punted a lot on first down and third down and we never practiced that," he said. "If a coach did that today, if I did that today, the press would hang me and the players would run me off."

The large crowd and the deafening noise it produced represented a peek into the future.

"It was one of the first real big Tiger Stadium games, with the great crowds and great noises that you experience nowadays in college football," Brewer said. "You couldn't hear yourself talk. I remember scouts saying, 'Man, it's unreal down there.'"

Cannon, a senior, was a favorite target of the fans' cheers. At 6-foot-1, 210 pounds, Cannon was a step faster and ten pounds heavier than most ballcarriers. The combination of immense physical talent and sheer determination made him the country's best running back.

"He was one of the biggest players at that time and one of the fastest, strongest players," Brewer said. "He was the first weightlifter that you had heard of. He was one of the first really publicized big-time players."

Cannon seemed destined for stardom. More than 50 schools recruited him out of Ioustrouma High School in Baton Rouge. He was the 1950s' version of O. J. Simpson: big, fast and talented.

It came as no surprise that people in Louisiana weren't about to let him slip out of the state and fortune was on their side. Cannon was involved in a minor scrape with the law and a judge who happened to be a strong LSU supporter put Cannon on probation with the stipulation that he report to the pardons board in Baton Rouge each week. LSU became Cannon's college choice.

What the Tigers got was a halfback who could run a 9.4 100-yard dash and was as strong as he was fast.

Postscript: LSU was ranked third by the Associated Press in a poll taken before bowl games. LSU lost to Mississippi, 21-0, in a rematch in the Sugar Bowl to finish 9-2. Brewer was personally assigned to shadow Cannon in the Sugar Bowl. "Everywhere he went, I went," Brewer said.

Mississippi finished 10-1 and was ranked second behind unbeaten Syracuse. Cannon, who won the Heisman Trophy, ended up rushing for 1,867 yards and scoring 154 points in his collegiate career. He was part of a controversial contract dispute, signing with both the Los Angeles Rams of the National Football League and the Houston Oilers of the American Football League. The Oilers went to court and won. Cannon helped Houston win AFL championships in 1960 and 1961. Cannon led the AFL in rushing with 948 yards in 1961.

Cannon, who also played for the Oakland Raiders and Kansas City Chiefs, was one of the 19 players who played in all ten AFL seasons. He rushed for 2,449 yards in 11 professional seasons. He later became an orthodontist in Baton Rouge.

Reference

1. *Sports Illustrated*, 9 November 1959.

USC's 42 Points Barely Enough
USC 42, Wisconsin 37 • January 1, 1963

The Rose Bowl matching top-ranked USC (10-0) and second-ranked Wisconsin (8-1) produced more thrills than the most spectacular of fireworks extravaganzas.

There were 11 touchdowns and 11 Rose Bowl records broken as USC survived a remarkable comeback to win, 42-37, before 98,698 fans in Pasadena, California. The game set a record for the highest-scoring Rose Bowl.

With seconds gone in the fourth quarter, Wisconsin trailed, 42–14. Who could have blamed the fans if they decided to leave early? Those who stayed were treated to a stirring rally orchestrated by Wisconsin quarterback Ron VanderKelen.

The Badgers scored 23 consecutive points in the final quarter, pulling to within five points. The game was not decided until a USC punt in the final seconds ran out the clock. By then, a relieved USC Coach John McKay celebrated his first national championship.

"When it was 42–14, the kids were congratulating each other on the sideline," McKay said afterward. "You would and I would. Wisconsin is a great offensive team, the best we've played."[1]

VanderKelen completed 33 of 48 passes for 401 yards and two touchdowns to share the game's most valuable player honors with USC quarterback Pete Beathard, who threw four touchdown passes. He completed 8 of 12 passes for 190 yards.

Two pass-catchers also enjoyed outstanding games. USC All-American end Hal Bedsole caught four passes for 101 yards and two touchdowns and Wisconsin All-American end Pat Richter caught 11 passes for 163 yards and one touchdown.

"It was such a great football game," VanderKelen said 28 years later. "I wish we had won, but we got as much praise for losing as they did for winning."

McKay had been on the hot seat after guiding the Trojans to records of 4-6 and 4-5-1 in his first two years as coach. So McKay understood the importance of showing the Trojan fans that he knew what he was doing in his first Rose Bowl.

"I think it was one of John McKay's great coaching jobs," said USC backup quarterback Craig Fertig in 1991.

The Trojans had some things in their favor. They had better speed and outstanding depth, particularly at quarterback with Beathard and backup Bill Nelsen. But the Trojans also were hurting on the offensive line. Starting tackle Marv Marinovich was ejected before the end of the first half for slugging a Wisconsin player. His usual replacement, Mike Gale, was sidelined with a neck injury. Another tackle, Gary Kirner, had injured himself a week before in a freak accident when he cut his ring finger.

"We were really hurting," McKay said.[2]

USC Coach John McKay. (Photo courtesy of USC Sports Information Department.)

The Trojans, who won their first national championship under McKay, had difficulty applying a pass rush to harass VanderKelen in the second half. Still, the Trojans could not have looked better on offense in opening their 42–14 lead. And their defense intercepted three VanderKelen passes.

USC took a 7–0 lead five minutes into the first quarter when

USC quarterback Pete Beathard. (Photo courtesy of USC Sports Information Department.)

78   USC 42, Wisconsin 37 (1963)

Beathard fired a 13-yard touchdown pass to Ron Butcher on a tackle-eligible play. Wisconsin soon tied the score, 7-7, on an 82-yard scoring drive, with Ralph Kurek scoring from the one.

USC expanded its lead to 21-7 at halftime on scoring runs of one yard by Ben Wilson and 25 yards by Ron Heller. Wisconsin was seriously hurt by a clipping penalty at the end of the first half that nullified a 30-yard VanderKelen touchdown pass.

The Trojans' lead grew to 28-7 on the first play of the second half. Beathard hit Bedsole with a short swing pass, and he ran 57 yards for a touchdown. VanderKelen replied with a 17-yard touchdown run before Beathard came back with touchdown passes of 23 yards to Bedsole and 13 yards to Fred Hill.

Down 42-14, the Badgers started to pass on almost every down. VanderKelen guided an 11-play, 80-yard drive, with Lou Holland scoring on a 13-yard run. USC fumbled on the first play following the kickoff, and VanderKelen hit Gary Kroner on a four-yard touchdown pass five plays later.

Then, after unsuccessful drives by both teams, a bad snap on a punt attempt sailed over the head of USC's Ernie Jones, and he was tackled in the end zone for a safety. The score was now USC 42, Wisconsin 30. It was becoming a wild fourth quarter.

Wisconsin took over the ball on the Trojans' 43 with less than three minutes left. VanderKelen teamed with Richter on a pair of completions, the last one covering 19 yards for a touchdown. Amazingly, with 1:19 left, Wisconsin had closed within 42-37.

The Badgers tried an onside kick, but USC's Pete Lubisich recovered. The Trojans then took time off the clock, losing 12 yards on three plays. Jones came on to punt, got off the kick and by the time the play had ended, time had expired.

Postscript: McKay coached USC through the 1975 season, compiling a record of 127-40-8. His teams played in eight Rose Bowls and won or shared four national championships. He left to become head coach of the Tampa Bay Buccaneers. Beathard played 10 years in the National Football League for four teams. Nelsen played 11 years in the NFL with the Pittsburgh Steelers and Cleveland Browns.

VanderKelen went unchosen in the National Football League draft, but he ended up signing with the Minnesota Vikings, for whom he played for six years. VanderKelen's Rose Bowl performance "opened a lot of doors," he said.

References

1. *Los Angeles Times*, 2 January 1963.
2. Ibid.

USC's Big Win Not So Rosy

USC 20, Notre Dame 17 • November 28, 1964

On a day in which USC produced one of its greatest victories, the Trojans also experienced one of their biggest disappointments.

USC bounced back from a seemingly hopeless 17–0 halftime deficit to post a 20–17 victory over Notre Dame, the nation's top-ranked team, before 83,840 fans at the Los Angeles Memorial Coliseum.

"It was the greatest comeback of all time," boasted USC quarterback Craig Fertig afterward.[1]

Fertig's 15-yard touchdown pass to Rod Sherman with 1:33 remaining in the game provided the winning points. Fertig rallied the Trojans by completing 10 of 14 passes for two touchdowns in the second half.

But the Trojans' exhilaration would not last long. Within hours of handing the Fighting Irish their first loss in both teams' regular-season finales, USC was stunned by the news that it was being passed over for a Rose Bowl invitation. Instead, Oregon State was named as the Pacific-8 Conference's representative by the conference's faculty athletic representatives.

USC and Oregon State finished the conference race the previous week tied for first place with 3-1 records. USC (7-3 overall) and Oregon State (8-2 overall) did not play each other during the season. When the Trojans and Beavers finished as co-champions, conference athletic representatives voted to wait until USC played Notre Dame before deciding which Pac-8 school would face Michigan in the Rose Bowl.

Believing a win over No. 1 Notre Dame would put them over the top in the Rose Bowl vote, the Trojans were disappointed and angry in losing out to Oregon State.

"It's the rankest injustice that ever occurred in the field of intercollegiate athletics," said USC Athletic Director Jess Hill afterward.[2]

"We all thought that if we beat Notre Dame, we'd go to the Rose Bowl," added Fertig. "I can't understand how they [conference representatives] could have voted the way they did."[3]

USC Coach John McKay was carried off the field after his team's rousing victory, but he declined to get carried away when discussing USC's snub. "I just hope Oregon State does a real fine job," said a diplomatic McKay. "It is a well-coached team and I hope it justifies the conference decision that they are better than we are."[4]

McKay was asked again in 1991 about the decision to send Oregon State to the Rose Bowl. He replied, "I don't look back," before adding sarcastically, "I think they loved [Oregon State Coach] Tommy Prothro."

USC started slowly in the first half against Notre Dame as the Fighting Irish moved the ball at will behind quarterback John Huarte, who consistently passed to end Jack Snow.

But it was a different story in the second half. The Trojans came out fired up and moved 66 yards after the opening kickoff, scoring on a one-yard run by Mike Garrett to make the score 17-7.

While Notre Dame's offense was beset with critical mistakes, USC maintained its offensive momentum. A Fertig-to-Fred Hill 23-yard touchdown pass in the fourth quarter cut the USC deficit to 17-13. Then with 2:10 remaining in the game, the Trojans got the ball back at Notre Dame's 40-yard line. Thirty-seven seconds later, USC took the lead for good as Sherman caught Fertig's touchdown pass despite Tony Carey hanging on his back.

Sherman had recommended to McKay that the Trojans run that pass pattern in which he delayed at the line of scrimmage before cutting downfield. "I told coach on the sidelines that I thought I could get a step on [Carey]," said Sherman, "and he told me to go ahead and take it into the huddle.

"[Carey] was right with me, but I had position on him. It was a perfect pass.... [Carey] didn't even have a chance at a tackle."[5]

While Fertig passed for 225 yards, the elusive Garrett led USC's ground game with 85 yards. "We never gave up," Garrett said. "We still thought we could win at halftime."[6]

"Coach McKay told us we could do it, to go out there and take the second-half kickoff to a touchdown and that would be all we needed," Fertig said. "We were moving the ball all along. Notre Dame is great, but we were confident."[7]

It was a crushing defeat for Notre Dame and its first-year Coach Ara Parseghian, who had turned the Fighting Irish around after a 2-7 season in 1963. Parseghian, who had just made the cover of *Time* magazine after his team was ranked No. 1 for the fourth straight week, took the defeat gracefully. But he acknowledged the importance of several breaks that went USC's way.

One of the biggest came after USC had scored its first touchdown to pare Notre Dame's lead to ten points. The Fighting Irish drove to the USC nine-yard line but came up empty when USC's John Lockwood recovered Huarte's wild pitchout intended for Bill Wolski. With Notre Dame still leading, 17-7, USC got another break early in the fourth quarter. Notre Dame's Joe Kantor plunged one yard for an apparent touchdown, but the score was nullified because of a holding penalty and the Fighting Irish wound up not scoring.

"I'm not disputing the penalty call," said Parseghian afterward, "but it's the weakest and most disastrous penalty in the book. If an offensive team holds, it has to go back 15 yards, but if the defensive team is holding, it loses only half the distance to the goal line when the ball is near the goal."[8]

Parseghian praised the Trojans, but added that "we didn't let down in the second half. We moved the ball pretty well, I thought."[9]

Not well enough, however, as the Fighting Irish failed to nail down the victory and their first national title in 15 years. Notre Dame would have to be content with a 9-1 season and a very near-miss national championship. And the Trojans would have to be content with a great comeback, even though it did not land them in the Rose Bowl.

Postscript: While USC sat out the bowl games, Oregon State was overwhelmed by Michigan, 34-7, in the Rose Bowl. In voting before the bowl games, the Irish finished third in the Associated Press national rankings behind No. 1 Alabama (10-0) and No. 2 Arkansas (10-0). Oregon State was eighth and USC tenth.

Huarte, who didn't play enough to win a letter the previous year as a junior, was a narrow Heisman Trophy winner over Tulsa quarterback Jerry Rhome. Snow, who caught 60 passes for 1,114 yards, finished fifth in the Heisman voting.

References

1. *Los Angeles Times*, 29 November 1964.
2. Ibid.

3. Ibid.
4. Ibid.
5. Ibid.
6. Ibid.
7. Ibid.
8. Ibid.
9. Ibid.

"Gutty Little Bruins" Rise Up

UCLA 14, Michigan State 12 • January 1, 1966

UCLA faced a mammoth challenge against Michigan State in the Rose Bowl. The difficulty of the Bruins' task was exemplified by the disparity in size of the teams' defensive lines.

Michigan State boasted 260-pound end Bubba Smith, who was so big he could smother running backs by simply falling on them. And he wasn't even the biggest Spartan. That honor went to 286-pound middle guard Harold Lucas. UCLA, by contrast, had linemen Alan Claman and Terry Donahue, who weighed 190 and 195 pounds, respectively. Lineman John Richardson was considered a Bruin giant at 231 pounds.

"We were given no chance," UCLA linebacker Don Manning said in 1991.

UCLA, however, showed up both the Spartans and the oddsmakers, who had installed the Bruins as 14-point underdogs. The Bruins scored two second-quarter touchdowns and held on for a 14–12 victory before a stunned crowd of 100,087 in Pasadena, California.

"If one less person had put out one less percent, we would have lost," UCLA Coach Tommy Prothro said.[1]

A massive infusion of self-confidence and determination was required by the Bruins to overcome Michigan State's advantages in size and talent. The same Michigan State team beat the Bruins, 13–3, in the season opener.

Prothro knew the Bruins (8-2-1) would have to gamble to win, and no play or strategy was held back.

Onside kicks, tackle-eligible plays, blitzes — everything was used.

Michigan State end Bubba Smith. (Photo courtesy of Michigan State Sports Information Department.)

Also important was a scouting report that revealed a Michigan State offensive tendency in short-yardage situations. In the end, though, the Bruins' refusal to accept defeat carried them to their first Rose Bowl victory in five attempts.

Jumping out to a 14–0 lead in the second quarter gave UCLA a

UCLA quarterback Gary Beban. (Photo courtesy of UCLA Sports Information Department.)

UCLA 14, Michigan State 12 (1966) 85

boost in confidence. First, the Bruins recovered a fumbled punt on the Spartans' six-yard line. Quarterback Gary Beban ran in from the one for the touchdown, with Kurt Zimmerman adding the conversion kick. Then UCLA's Dallas Grider recovered an onside kick on the Michigan State 42. The frustrated Spartans immediately gave up a 21-yard run to Mel Farr. Beban followed with a pass down the middle to Kurt Altenberg, who took the ball to the one. Again, Beban went in for the score, with Zimmerman adding the kick.

For three quarters, Michigan State (10-1) struggled on offense. It wasn't as if the Spartans were making mistakes – UCLA's defense kept hustling and playing Michigan State tendencies. Twice in the third quarter, the Bruins halted Michigan State drives on fourth down.

But even the Bruins realized the Spartans would eventually score. They weren't No. 1 in the country and 10-0 for nothing. Michigan State started beating up on the Bruins in the fourth quarter.

Midway through the final quarter, Michigan State fullback Bob Apisa raced 38 yards for a touchdown. Michigan State tried to go for the two-point conversion with a fake kick, but quarterback Steve Juday threw an interception under heavy pressure. The score was Bruins 14, Spartans 6.

Michigan State then stopped the Bruins, forcing a punt. The Spartans took over on their 42, and it was inevitable the game would come down to a final drive. With Juday and Jim Raye alternating at quarterback as Coach Duffy Daugherty sent in plays, the Spartans drove downfield. With 31 seconds left and the ball on the one, Juday dived in for the touchdown. That set the stage for the decisive two-point conversion attempt.

Daughterty used Raye as his quarterback and had the team line up on the left side to provide more running room right. Raye took the snap, ran to his right and pitched back to the 220-pound Apisa, who set his sights on the end zone. He never made it. First, UCLA's Jim Colletto met him at the three, then Bob Stiles, the game's most valuable player, charged in with a fierce blow, using his head and shoulders. Apisa was stopped short of the end zone. Stiles lay on the ground stunned by the impact and exhausted by the emotional wringer he and his teammates had just gone through.

UCLA Trainer Ducky Drake came in from the sideline to examine Stiles. According to Stiles, the conversation went something like this:

"Bobby, Bobby, are you all right?" Drake asked.

Michigan State Coach Duffy Daugherty. (Photo courtesy of Michigan State Sports Information Department.)

"Ducky, move away," Stiles replied. "I'm listening to the applause."

The Bruins had pulled off the biggest upset of the season and the players knew it.

"They would have beaten us four out of five times," said Stiles, a defensive back who contributed two interceptions. "We shouldn't have been on the field with them on talent alone."

Stiles typified UCLA's winning spirit that made up for a shortage in talent. It was Stiles' only season at UCLA after transferring from Long Beach City College and Mississippi. But his attitude was to do anything to help his team to win. And he, like many of his teammates, was a student of football.

"Something like that sounds ludicrous," Stiles said, "but we had a little more knowledge of the game [than Michigan State]."

What UCLA also had was a brilliant teacher and strategist in Pro-thro. He had left his head coaching position at Oregon State to come to UCLA and then he prevailed in the Rose Bowl in his rookie year as Bruin head coach.

Postscript: Michigan State finished second and UCLA fourth in the final Associated Press rankings. Prothro coached UCLA through the 1970 season, compiling a record of 41-18-3 before becoming head coach of the Los Angeles Rams and San Diego Chargers. Beban went on to win the Heisman Trophy as a senior in 1967. Farr became a star running back for the Detroit Lions. Smith was the first player taken in the 1967 National Football League draft and became an All-Pro with the Balti-more Colts.

The valiant UCLA effort against Michigan State brought forth the term "Gutty Little Bruins" to describe a UCLA undersized and over-achieving team. Three UCLA players—Donahue (UCLA), Colletto (Purdue) and Steve Butler (L.A. Valley College)—went on to become college head coaches.

Reference

1. *Sports Illustrated*, 10 January 1966.

Notre Dame Settles for Its Comeback Tie

Notre Dame 10, Michigan State 10 • November 19, 1966

Debate raged over who deserved to be the No. 1–rated team in the country before Notre Dame and Michigan State took to the East Lan-sing, Michigan, field to try to hammer out a clear-cut answer.

And after 60 minutes of big-time collisions, the answer appeared just as vague as before.

No. 1 Notre Dame and No. 2 Michigan State played to a 10–10 tie before 80,001 frigid fans, many of whom were booing at the end when Notre Dame appeared to be content with a come-from-behind deadlock by keeping the ball on the ground.

Notre Dame rallied from a ten-point deficit with a 34-yard, second-quarter touchdown pass from reserve quarterback Coley O'Brien and a 24-yard field goal by Joe Azzaro on the first play of the fourth quarter. But the Fighting Irish were not going to do anything rash when they got the ball at their 30-yard line with 1:15 remaining in the game. Six Notre Dame running plays later, the game was over, but the second-guessing of Irish Coach Ara Parseghian's decision to play it safe was just beginning.

"I simply wasn't going to give away cheaply the tie our crippled team had fought so hard to obtain," said Parseghian afterward. "If we'd been in the middle of the field, it might have been different. But with the ball on our 35, I wasn't going to risk a pass interception because of the great field-goal kicking ability of Michigan State's (Dick) Kenney.

"After all, the Spartans almost lost the game that way a few plays earlier when we intercepted and were in field-goal position."[1]

On that occasion, Notre Dame had an opportunity to take a three-point lead after Tom Schoen made his second successive interception of a Jimmy Raye pass, running the ball from midfield to the Michigan State 18. But after the Spartans' defense stiffened and forced the Irish backward, Azzaro's 41-yard field-goal try sailed wide.

Notre Dame's last-minute conservative play-calling contrasted with Michigan State's desperate effort to pull out a victory. After Azzaro's missed field goal, Michigan State mobilized an offense that tried to pull out the stops to drive downfield. The Spartans even ran on fourth down from their 31-yard line to maintain possession. Eventually, however, Michigan State was forced to punt with little more than a minute remaining.

But even with Notre Dame back in possession, Michigan State didn't waver from its frenzied drive to win. While Notre Dame ran the ball, Michigan State called time-outs after each of the Irish's first three plays. However, Notre Dame all but sealed a tie after racking up a first down on its 40.

It was a tie Notre Dame accepted, but not one the Irish really wanted, Parseghian stressed.

"After we got that field goal on the first play of the final quarter, I certainly gave no consideration to a tie," Parseghian said. "I felt we had a good chance, but it just didn't work out that way.

"At the end, I had to feel that any team that would come back after

Notre Dame quarterback Terry Hanratty. (Photo courtesy of Notre Dame Sports Information Department.)

being 10–0 behind, after losing its quarterback, its best runner and its No. 1 center, deserved not to lose. I am awfully proud of this team."[2]

Notre Dame quarterback Terry Hanratty left for good early in the game when he was tackled by linebacker Charlie Thornhill and 283-pound defensive end Bubba Smith fell on him. Halfback Nick Eddy reinjured his shoulder when he slipped getting off the train at Lansing, but he might not have played anyway. And center George Goeddeke suffered an ankle sprain in the first quarter. The injuries did not end there. Eddy's backup, Bob Gladieux, sprained his knee in the second half.

"The criticism I still feel was unjust," said Parseghian in 1991. "At issue is simply the press. None other than (*Sports Illustrated's*) Dan Jenkins took issue with the play-calling in the last minute of the game. We've got a newspaperman telling us what we should do, what we should have done in the last minute.

"I run the ball club for the whole season and all of a sudden the last minute of the critical game, I'm getting told what I should have done. No one knew better than I what was best for the team. We weren't going to give the game away.

"They had a helluva field-goal kicker. The wind going with them. I had the starting quarterback on the bench with no starting center and no starting halfback (all injured). I had a bunch of injuries. There was a lot of criticism and I feel to this day unjustly."

Michigan State Coach Duffy Daugherty, for his part, refused to be drawn into the play-it-safe controversy afterward, declining to criticize the Irish strategy. "That's not my area," Daugherty said. "Anything I would say could be construed as a criticism."[3]

But Daugherty said the tie did not diminish in his mind how he felt about the Spartans. "We think we are the best," he said. "I don't think anyone can say Notre Dame is better than us. We both deserve the national championship."[4]

Notre Dame standout wide receiver Jim Seymour defended Parseghian's decision. "What people don't realize is that we couldn't throw the ball because they had set up a specific defense to stop the pass," remembered Seymour, who uncharacteristically failed to catch a pass.

"Our quarterback was so run-down because of his diabetic problem that he couldn't throw the ball more than 10 yards. And they were really set up for it. So why throw the ball for an interception and really hang yourself? Ara's been questioned many times about that decision. . . . But there was nothing else he could do under the circumstances."[5]

O'Brien, who required two insulin shots a day to keep his diabetes in check, passed 19 times, completing 7 for 102 yards.

Michigan State (9-0-1) took a 7-0 lead early in the second quarter on a four-yard run by fullback Regis Cavender. Wide receiver Gene Washington, who hauled in five passes for 123 yards, helped set up the score with a brilliant 42-yard diving reception of a Raye pass. The Spartans added a 37-yard field goal in the second quarter from Kenney to increase their lead to 10-0.

But the Irish (8-0-1) responded before the half ended to make it 10-7. A 39-yard kickoff return by Tom Quinn gave Notre Dame excellent field position close to midfield. Then O'Brien completed two short passes before the sophomore teamed with Gladieux on a 34-yard touchdown pass.

"That was something of a turning point," said Daugherty about Notre Dame's late first-half score.[6]

In the statistical battle, Michigan State finished slightly ahead, enjoying an edge in first downs, 13 to 10; rushing, 142 yards to 91; passing, 142 yards to 128; and total yards, 284 to 219. But the Spartans could do no better than even in the all-important scoring column.

Postscript: The Notre Dame game marked Michigan State's season finale. The Big Ten champion Spartans did not play in the Rose Bowl game because of the conference's no-repeat rule. Notre Dame overwhelmed USC, 51-0, to end its season at 9-0-1. The Fighting Irish were named the national champions in both the Associated Press and United Press International voting; Michigan State finished second in both polls.

References

1. *Los Angeles Times*, 20 November 1966.
2. Ibid.
3. Ibid.
4. Ibid.
5. *Notre Dame 1990 Football Press Guide.*
6. *Los Angeles Times*, 20 November 1966.

USC, Simpson Sprint Past UCLA

USC 21, UCLA 20 • November 18, 1967

An electrifying sprint by junior tailback O. J. Simpson sparked USC on its run to the Roses as the Trojans scored a 21–20 victory over top-ranked UCLA.

In a game filled with big plays, Simpson turned in the biggest of them all to lead the third-ranked Trojans to a berth in the Rose Bowl. Simpson's 64-yard touchdown run allowed USC to overcome a 20–14 deficit in a game that drew 90,772 fans to the Los Angeles Memorial Coliseum.

Simpson provided the winning edge early in the fourth quarter. The Trojans, experiencing difficulties moving the ball, faced third down and eight on their 36-yard line with little more than ten minutes remaining in the game. Toby Page had replaced Steve Sogge at quarterback. Simpson was tired, having carried the ball again and again.

Page called a pass play, but as he arrived at the line of scrimmage, he saw a UCLA linebacker drop off to play pass defense. He called an audible, "Red 23-Blast." Simpson got the ball and plowed ahead looking simply to pick up a first down. Guard Steve Lehmer and tackle Mike Taylor opened a hole, Simpson shot through and then discovered he might have room to use his 9.4 sprinter speed.

Like a jet fighter suddenly igniting its afterburner, Simpson took off. He veered to the left sideline, angled back toward the middle, then to his right and ran 64 yards for a touchdown, lifting USC (9-1) into a 21–20 lead.

UCLA Coach Tommy Prothro said in 1991 that he decided before the game that he would rather have the Trojans pass on third down than let Simpson run, but the Bruins failed to follow the plan on Simpson's dash.

"Two things happened on the run that were unfortunate," Prothro said. "One was our end dropped off [into pass coverage] as he had been doing all year and he forgot not to do it, so we didn't have a man in there that should have been. Second, I made a mistake in that probably our best defensive football player (linebacker Don Manning) had a bad shoulder ... and he assured me he was in good shape and wanted to play.

"But you look at the picture of it, and the guy [Simpson] went by on his right side, which was his bad shoulder, and he reached cross-handed and tried to tackle him with his left hand reaching across, so I had the wrong man in the game."

Simpson rushed for 177 yards in 30 carries. It was Prothro's strategy to do everything possible to tire Simpson out. The plan was to act polite and help him off the turf the minute a whistle blew to keep him from resting.

"At the beginning of the game, it was irritating because every time I got the ball, they grabbed me," said Simpson in 1991. "You hit the ground and . . . they pull you up.

"They were grabbing me by the belt, by the arm, by the shoulder pads. They had me off the ground before I knew what was going on. I must admit late in the game, I was saying, 'Come on, guys.'"

The Rose Bowl bid from the Pacific-8 Conference was on the line, but there was more at stake. UCLA had the nation's top senior in quarterback Gary Beban and USC had the fastest rising star in Simpson and the two battled to improve their Heisman Trophy position.

Beban, playing with bruised ribs, acquitted himself magnificently. He completed 16 of 24 passes for 301 yards and two touchdowns. His 20-yard touchdown pass to Dave Nuttall early in the fourth quarter gave UCLA (7-1-1) a 20-14 lead. The point-after kick by Zenon Andrusyshyn was blocked and later proved costly to the Bruins.

Trying to put the game in perspective, Jerry Long, UCLA's defensive coach, said afterward, "A loss like this can make you sick, but I don't feel that way. These kids were all heart in there. They have a great team. And so do we. And that Simpson. He's probably one of the greatest backs who ever lived, especially with all those monsters in front of him. But you can't take anything away from Beban. They couldn't stop him either."[1]

But Beban was overshadowed by Simpson, who in 1991 labeled USC's victory over UCLA and his long dash as his greatest football thrill. "Without a doubt, it was my favorite game," Simpson said. "It

Opposite: Southern California halfback O. J. Simpson breaks into the clear on a 64-yard gallop for USC's third touchdown which gave the Trojans a 21-20 victory over UCLA. At left is center Dick Almon (66) with end Ron Drake (83) on the ground. Just to left of Simpson is Coach John McKay of USC. UCLA player at right is Sandy Green. (Photo courtesy of USC Sports Information Department.)

was because of what was at stake and when the game was over, we were the national champions.

"It was the first time I felt that kind of euphoria. It was the culmination of the most exciting year of my life. In January, I was a kid living with his mother in an attic in San Francisco.

"That's how I came into 1967. I left 1967 having run on indoor and outdoor NCAA track championship teams, had a world record in the 440-yard relay, got married that summer and was the Associated Press and UPI player of the year."

Simpson had arrived at USC only nine months earlier as a transfer from City College of San Francisco, for which he scored 54 touchdowns in two seasons. Against UCLA, the 6-foot-1, 202-pound Simpson highlighted his junior season by pulling off one of the most memorable runs in college football history.

Postscript: USC beat Indiana, 14–3, in the Rose Bowl to finish 10–1 and as the national champion. UCLA finished 7-2-1 and ranked tenth by United Press International.

Beban won the Heisman Trophy with 1,968 points, edging out Simpson, who garnered 1,722 points. Beban ended his collegiate career by rushing and passing for 5,358 yards and 58 touchdowns. He was selected in the first round by the Los Angeles Rams in the 1968 draft, traded to the Washington Redskins and retired after the 1970 season.

Simpson led the nation in rushing during his junior season, gaining 1,543 yards in ten games. He also threw three touchdown passes. The following season, Simpson won the Heisman Trophy. He finished with 3,423 yards rushing and 36 touchdowns in 21 games at USC.

The Buffalo Bills made Simpson the first player selected in the 1969 National Football League draft. In 1973, he became the first NFL player to rush for more than 2,000 yards (2,003) and set records with 11 games of 100 or more yards rushing and a single-game record of 250 yards rushing.

In 11 NFL seasons, Simpson rushed for 11,236 yards and scored 61 touchdowns. He retired in 1979 and was inducted into the Pro Football Hall of Fame.

Reference

1. *Los Angeles Times,* 19 November 1967.

Texas A&M's Stallings
"Bears Down" Against His Teacher
Texas A&M 20, Alabama 16 • January 1, 1968

One of the greatest tributes for a teacher is to see a former student become successful. Perhaps that's why the always-competitive Paul "Bear" Bryant was so gracious in defeat after his former pupil, Gene Stallings, guided Texas A&M to a 20–16 upset over Alabama before 75,504 fans in the Cotton Bowl in Dallas.

Bryant went up to the Texas A&M coach, lifted him off the turf and carried him half the distance of the field. "He's a strong scamp, isn't he?" said Stallings afterward.[1]

It was an emotional moment and revealed the special bond between teacher and pupil. As Stallings recalled 23 years later, "I really wanted my players exposed to Coach Bryant more than anything else. When the game was over, he came into our dressing room and visited with our players for a while. I appreciated that. It was one game I remember very fondly."

Stallings had played for Bryant at Texas A&M in the 1950s, then was his assistant coach for seven years at Alabama. Now he was head coach at Texas A&M, trying to outsmart a man who already was a coaching legend. It was almost a final test for Stallings, and his Texas A&M players sensed the importance of playing Alabama.

"We know that's what our program had been built on because Coach Stallings had been with Coach Bryant for so many years," Aggies defensive back Curley Hallman said in 1991. "We understood our coach was playing the legendary Coach Bryant."

Although Alabama, with an 8-1-1 record, was the favorite and had more talent, Texas A&M was on a roll. The Aggies started the season 0-4 but hadn't lost since. They won the Southwest Conference championship and were on a six-game winning streak.

As Hallman said, "We hung together during the difficult times and each week we won, we got a little bit stronger, became a little closer and got to the point where we were a bunch of kids who didn't think we could lose."

At the same time, there were warning signs that Alabama might be ready to take a fall. "Coach Bryant wasn't really satisfied with practice. He kept telling the assistant coaches we better get off our tails because that other bunch is hungry and wants to play," said Assistant Coach Dude Hennessey in 1991.

No Texas A&M player was more excited than Hallman, who grew up five miles from the Alabama campus in Northport. Bryant didn't offer him a scholarship, so this was his chance to show that Bryant had misjudged him. He fulfilled his mission by intercepting two passes from Alabama quarterback Ken Stabler.

"It's a wonder he didn't intercept four passes," Hennessey said. "He'd been ready to play and stayed ready to play. He was ready to play another game after that game got over. Old Curley, his heart was bigger than his body and he didn't know anything but full speed and he could run all day."

Texas A&M quarterback Edd Hargett passed for two touchdowns in the first half, giving the Aggies a 13-10 lead. He finished 11 of 22 for 143 yards. Then Texas A&M got the decisive touchdown in the third quarter when fullback Wendell Housley broke off runs of 13 and 20 yards, the latter for a touchdown.

Stabler did his best to keep the Crimson Tide in the game, completing 16 of 26 passes for 179 yards. He also scored two touchdowns. But Stabler threw three interceptions and Alabama also lost two fumbles.

"If Stallings had been on our side instead of me, he would still be the winning coach," Bryant said afterwards. "He did a better job with his team than I did with ours. Errors belong to the coach. If you do a good job teaching, you don't make errors. I always hate to lose, but if I have to lose, I'd rather it be to them."[2]

The victory completed a rags-to-riches season for Texas A&M, which somehow overcame its seemingly disastrous beginning to return to the Cotton Bowl after a 26-year absence.

"To play one of those great, mature programs like Alabama and to beat them in the Cotton Bowl and win seven in a row was the climax of a great season for a bunch of old guys who never gave up," Hallman said.

As for the legacy of Bryant, who coached for 38 years, the last in 1982, Hennessey said, "He wanted you to give the best you had. You don't have to show them how smart you are or how intelligent you are. He just thought you had to have a lot of enthusiasm."

Postscript: History would repeat itself 22 years later when Hallman faced Stallings, his former teacher. Hallman was head coach of Southern Mississippi in 1990 and Stallings was in his first season as head coach at Alabama. Hallman's team won, 27–24.

Stallings was 27-45-1 in seven years as Texas A&M head coach. He was fired after the 1971 season and went on to become an assistant for Coach Tom Landry of the Dallas Cowboys and head coach of the St. Louis Cardinals. He took over as coach of Alabama in 1990.

Hallman never played football after college and became head coach at Southern Mississippi and then at LSU in 1991. Hargett was a 16th-round selection of the New Orleans Saints and played four seasons there and one with the Houston Oilers. Stabler became a standout for the Oakland Raiders from 1970–79, and led his team to a 32–14 victory over the Minnesota Vikings in the 1977 Super Bowl. He was a four-time Pro Bowl selection and passed for 19,078 yards in his professional career.

References

1. The Associated Press, 2 January 1968.
2. Ibid.

Harvard's Champi Enjoys a Dream Performance
Harvard 29, Yale 29 • November 23, 1968

For Frank Champi, it literally was a dream come true.

Champi, Harvard's second-string quarterback, came off the bench and turned in a scintillating performance against Yale in both teams' final game of the season.

With Harvard trailing, 22–0, before 40,280 fans at Harvard Stadium in Cambridge, Massachusetts, Champi led Harvard back with three touchdown passes, including two in the final 42 seconds. Harvard scored 16 points in those final 42 seconds, converting both two-point conversion tries, to finish in a 29–29 tie.

Champi's two-point conversion pass to Pat Varney with time expired allowed Harvard to post its first unbeaten season since 1920 at 8-0-1 and claim a share of the Ivy League championship with Yale, which also finished at 8-0-1.

It was a scenario few could have predicted. Yet Champi, a 5-foot-11 junior, hardly seemed caught by surprise.

"It's been a strange day from the beginning," said Champi afterward. "I'm an intuitive guy and when I woke up this morning, I was sort of in a dream. It felt like something great was going to happen to me.

"Then when I got here, I still felt strange. It didn't feel like I was here but someplace else. I still don't feel like I'm here. It's all very strange."[1]

It was an unlikely ending considering Champi had completed only 5 of 12 passes for 46 yards during the season before he replaced starter George Lalich late in the first half.

"The whole week preceding the game seemed strange," said Champi in 1991. "There just seemed to be something in the air. Even one of my roommates said he had a dream or two about the game. I thought that indicated something, a sign that something was going to happen.

"I'm a believer in hunches and signs and, not to sound bizarre, I have a certain quality or feel for certain events. If nothing happened, of course, I would have thought it was just that the nights were clear and the air smelled clean."

Champi said that he believed Harvard Coach John Yovicsin played a hunch by inserting him abruptly before the first half ended with Harvard trailing by 22 points.

"I hadn't played much all year," Champi said, "and it seemed like a desperate move."

Champi, however, delivered in "The Game" (the annual Harvard-Yale contest), completing 6 of 15 passes for 82 yards and three touchdowns. With 39 seconds left in the first half, he threw a 15-yard touchdown pass to Bruce Freeman to allow the Crimson to close within 22–6.

Harvard narrowed its deficit to 22–13 in the third quarter when fullback Gus Crim scored on a one-yard run. But Yale quarterback Brian Dowling, who closed his career by setting eight school records, scored from five yards out to boost Yale into a 29–13 lead with only 10:44 remaining. It was Dowling's record running touchdown to go with his two touchdown passes. In the second quarter, Dowling had thrown a three-yard touchdown pass to Calvin Hill, allowing the running back to pass Albie Booth and set a Yale record for points (144) in a career.

After Yale moved out to its 16-point fourth-quarter lead, its fans waved handkerchiefs and screamed, "You're No. 2," across the field. For Harvard and its reserve quarterback, an Ivy League championship appeared to be out of reach.

But Harvard captain Vic Gatto said the team found incentive and inspiration from the antics of the Yale fans. "When they started waving those white hankies and yelling," Gatto said, "it got to us."[2]

Undaunted, Champi drove his team 86 yards in nine plays, giving Harvard its third touchdown with a 16-yard pass to Freeman with 42 seconds remaining. Champi's pass for the two-point conversion fell incomplete, but Harvard got another chance when Yale was called for interference. Crim then ran in for the two-point conversion to bring Harvard within eight points, giving Harvard hope.

An onside kick was now a foregone conclusion. But that probability somehow escaped Yale, which lined up in a normal 5-4-2 formation for the kickoff. Yale's Brad Lee bobbled the onside kick and was swarmed on by a host of Harvard tacklers. Harvard's Bill Kelly recovered at Yale's 49.

Champi then scrambled for 14 yards and was pulled down by the facemask, a 15-yard infraction that brought Harvard to Yale's 20 with 26 seconds remaining. After two incompletions, Crim ran to the six on a draw play. With 14 seconds left, Champi was sacked for a two-yard loss.

Now with three seconds remaining, Harvard was on Yale's eight-yard line. There was time for only one more play from scrimmage.

A strong pass rush forced Champi to move left, then right before he sailed a pass toward the left corner of the end zone.

Gatto made the reception and Harvard miraculously was only two points behind with a conversion attempt remaining.

"By this time," Champi said, "I was so tired that I wasn't even nervous."[3]

Champi's dream ending came when he hit Varney for the two-point conversion as Yale finished in a nightmarish tie.

Postscript: Champi quit Harvard's team after two games of his senior season with Harvard 1-1 at the time. "I was tired of football," he said. "I had played since junior high on and I always was fully dedicated to football. I just felt I was missing something in the fall.

"It was the height of the Vietnam War and I didn't think football was that important and I didn't think I would go on and play after college ball."

Hill was a first-round draft choice of the Dallas Cowboys, with whom he became a standout running back. He rushed for 5,009 yards for the Cowboys from 1979 to 1984 and finished with 6,083 yards in his National Football League career.

References

1. *Sports Illustrated*, 2 December 1968.
2. Ibid.
3. Ibid.

A Royal Gamble Pays Off
Texas 15, Arkansas 14 • December 6, 1969

Rarely has a game received more pregame hype on a national scale and then lived up to its billing as this showdown between top-ranked Texas and No. 2–ranked Arkansas in Fayetteville, Arkansas. Both teams entered the game 9-0.

Months before, ABC executive Roone Arledge convinced the schools to move the game from October 18 to the first Saturday in December, when the regular season had already ended for most NCAA Division I teams. Arledge's foresight created a dream matchup for the national title.

Millions watched on television and celebrities showed up en masse to see the game of the year. President Richard Nixon was there, as was top adviser Henry Kissinger. Future President George Bush was there. The Rev. Billy Graham was there. About the only big name missing was Elvis Presley, and he met Texas quarterback James Street in Las Vegas a few months later to discuss the game.

Arkansas, coached by Frank Broyles, held a 14–0 lead going into the fourth quarter. The Razorbacks had shut down the Longhorns' famed

Texas quarterback James Street. (Photo courtesy of Texas Sports Information Department.)

wishbone attack that featured Street, Steve Worster at fullback and Jim Bertelsen and Ted Koy at halfback. But Street, who entered the game 18-0 as a starting quarterback, ignited Texas by scrambling 42 yards for a touchdown on the first play of the fourth quarter, then adding the two-point conversion on an option run to make the score 14-8.

Later, Texas Coach Darrell Royal made a big gamble that turned the game around. With Texas facing a fourth-and-three situation on its 43 with a little more than four minutes left, Royal called for a rare Longhorn pass play. Street fired the ball to tight end Randy Peschel for a 44-yard reception. Two plays later, Bertelsen scored from the two with 3:58 left, and Happy Feller's conversion gave Texas a 15-14 victory before a crowd of 44,000.

It was a startling ending to a game that was played with incredible intensity. Here was Royal, the man who disdained passing, risking everything by calling a surprise pass at the most crucial moment of the season's biggest game.

"Had it been unsuccessful," Royal recalled 22 years later, "it would have been the most criticized call of all time. They would never have forgiven me for it."

In Royal's mind, he had no choice but to try the pass to Peschel.

"We hadn't moved the ball all day long," he said. "We hadn't made three or four plays that gained more than four yards. They had confused us with a defense we hadn't worked against. It was a clever maneuver. They flashed their tackle down and looped their linebacker out. Our linemen simply didn't block anyone. I felt we had to get something big."

Street came to the sideline, grabbed a phone and talked with offensive coordinator Emory Bellard in the press box. Also listening in was Royal. Everybody knew the game was on the line, creating a moment to remember.

"All three of us are on the phone talking," Street said in 1991. "Emory and myself both wanted to run a play that set the formation to the wide side, where they had been overshifted, and run a counter option to the short side.

"We're giving our opinion what would work and out of nowhere Coach Royal says, 'I'll tell you what we're going to run. We're going to run, right 53 veer pass.' At the same time, the defensive coordinator, Coach Mike Campbell, is standing there in the huddle listening to us and he turns around and starts hollering. 'Defense get ready!' So I don't

Texas running back Jim Bertelsen. (Photo courtesy of Texas Sports Information Department.)

Texas Coach Darrell Royal. (Photo courtesy of Texas Sports Information Department.)

know whether Campbell had seen me pass or was worried about the play itself."

Royal's pass selection was not a spontaneous decision.

"I had talked to our tight end at halftime," Royal said, "and he said they weren't paying any attention to him when he released downfield. I had that catalogued in the back of my mind."

The play succeeded, but not as easily as Peschel had suggested. In fact, he was double-covered.

"As it happened, they had their safety and halfback all over him," Royal said. "There were six hands up there and two of them belonged to us. It was like putting the ball through a keyhole, but it got to him and he caught it."

"It was one of those deals if you run it 100 times, I couldn't have thrown the ball any better and he couldn't have made any better catch," said Street.

On the play after the catch, Koy broke loose on an 11-yard run to take the ball to the two. It was redemption for Koy, who had fumbled twice before. Then Bertelsen did the rest, using his power to get into the end zone.

The game turned out as hard-fought as predicted. Royal had said before the game: "They're gonna come after us with their eyes pulled up like BBs. And they'll be defending every foot as if Frank Broyles has told 'em there's a 350-foot drop just behind 'em into a pile of rocks."[1]

What Arkansas had not counted on was Royal's surprise fourth-down call.

"In the midst of probably the biggest game he ever coached and I ever played in, out of nowhere he says, 'Right 53 veer pass,' which is a play we had not run all year long. I don't know what possesses somebody to do that," Street said.

Ask Royal, and the answer is simple: "You can't base it on calling something that would be acceptable if it doesn't work. That would be a gutless way out."

Postscript: The Texas-Arkansas game was seen by more than 17 million people on television. It produced an 18.2 rating and whopping 50 share on ABC, meaning half the TV sets in America were tuned to the game.

Texas won the national championship after finishing 11-0, including a 21–17 victory over Notre Dame in the Cotton Bowl. The Longhorns' wishbone attack gained 3,630 yards on the ground during the season. Bertelsen and Koy went on to play in the National Football League, with Worster playing in the Canadian Football League. Royal coached at Texas from 1957–76, recording a mark of 167-47-5 while winning three national championships. He became the Texas athletic director for two years after he retired from coaching. Street never played professional football. He went into the insurance business in Austin, Texas. Arkansas lost to Mississippi, 27-22, in the Sugar Bowl to finish 9-2 and ranked No. 7.

Reference

1. *Sports Illustrated*, 15 December 1969.

Notre Dame Runs into
Dead End Against Texas

Texas 21, Notre Dame 17 • January 1, 1970

Darrell Royal doesn't like testimonials about his coaching ability, but the simple fact is that he had as much to do with Texas going 11-0 and winning the national championship in the 1969 season as his players did.

Sometimes coaches receive too much or too little credit in the success of their teams, but Royal's daring, innovative decisions helped the Longhorns win their two most important games, a 15–14 triumph over previously unbeaten Arkansas and a 21–17 victory over Notre Dame in the Cotton Bowl in Dallas.

A crowd of 73,000 came to see whether Notre Dame, playing in its first bowl game in 45 years, could spoil the Longhorns' bid for a national title.

Texas refused to become tentative. Royal had his team gambling on fourth downs, passing up easy field goals and playing as if there were no tomorrow. It was a wise move considering that Notre Dame Coach Ara Parseghian had the Fighting Irish primed for an upset.

Notre Dame quarterback Joe Theismann gave his team a 10-0 lead in the second quarter when he fired a 54-yard touchdown pass to Tom Gatewood. Texas, behind its bruising wishbone attack, rallied for a 14–10 lead on touchdown runs of one yard by Jim Bertelsen and three yards by Ted Koy.

Notre Dame regained the lead at 17–14 with 6:52 remaining in the fourth quarter when Theismann teamed with Jim Yoder on a 24-yard touchdown pass. Now it was up to the Longhorns to put up or shut up.

Texas quarterback James Street then directed his team on a 17-play, 76-yard drive, using 5:44 on the clock. Twice on fourth down, Street gambled to keep the drive alive. On fourth and two from the Notre Dame 20, Street pitched to Koy for a two-yard gain and a first down. On fourth and two from the Notre Dame 10, Street connected with Cotton Speyrer, who made a diving catch at the two.

Notre Dame's defense tried to hold. Bertelsen picked up a yard, then was limited to no gain. On third down, Street faked, then pitched the ball to reserve halfback Billy Dale, who plunged in for the winning touchdown with 68 seconds left.

Theismann had one final opportunity to rally the Irish, but Texas defensive back Tom Campbell intercepted his pass with 28 seconds left.

The heroes and standout performers abounded. Texas fullback Steve Worster rushed for 155 yards in 20 carries. Bertelsen powered his way for 81 yards in 18 carries. Street completed 6 of 11 passes for 107 yards and rushed for 31 yards. Theismann was terrific, completing 17 of 27 for 231 yards.

But Royal's willingness to hold nothing back was the real key to the victory. In the December 6, 1969 game against No. 2–ranked Arkansas, Royal made the decision to have Street throw on fourth and three from his 43 with about four minutes remaining. It resulted in a 44- yard gain and later the winning touchdown. Against Notre Dame, Royal's complete confidence in Street resulted in another victory.

Regarding his pass to Speyrer, Street said afterward, "If I had drilled the ball, it might have been a touchdown, but me being the great passer that I am, the ball just barely got to him. I knew he would go for six points — Coach Royal never plays for a tie. He plays to win."[1]

Royal's ability to recognize the strengths and limitations of his players demonstrated his greatness as a coach.

"He kind of reminds me of a president," said Worster in 1991. "He's very well-organized, smart and knows football well. He surrounded himself with an outstanding coaching staff."

It was Royal's decision to put in the run-oriented wishbone attack the previous season, enabling Texas to conclude the 1969 season with a 20-game winning streak.

"What made it special was it was a first," Worster said about the wishbone. "The offense didn't exist before. The biggest problem was trying to figure out a way to defense it. The offense is designed so that whatever you do defensively, we had an adjustment to counter it with the triple option."

Worster, 6-foot-1 and 220 pounds, was perfectly suited for fullback in the wishbone. He had the power and toughness to plow ahead at full speed.

"The whole design of the offense was to get the fullback up to the line as quickly as possible so they could put the ball into my belly and ride me through the line and go to the next option if the quarterback didn't hand it off," Worster said.

"I loved it. What we had before was an I-formation, where the tail-back ran all the time. This gave everyone an option and everyone a chance to run the ball."

After defeating Notre Dame, Texas players were suddenly celebrities. "We were kings," Worster said.

Former President Lyndon Johnson greeted Royal in the locker room, and President Richard Nixon called by phone to congratulate the Longhorns.

But Royal was not in a mood to celebrate. He was more relieved than excited. "This was tough," he said. "I suffered through the entire game. I just feel like I ache."[2]

Postscript: Texas went on to win its first ten games of the 1970 season, then lost to Notre Dame, 24–11, in a Cotton Bowl rematch that ended the Longhorns' winning streak at 30 games. Royal retired from coaching after the 1976 season with a record of 167-47-5 and three national titles at Texas. The Longhorns rushed for 3,630 yards in the 1969 season.

Theismann was runner-up to Stanford's Jim Plunkett in the Heisman Trophy balloting the following season. Theismann enjoyed a successful career in the Canadian Football League and later with the Washington Redskins. Notre Dame finished 8-2-1 and ranked fifth in the Associated Press ratings.

References

1. The Associated Press, 2 January 1970.
2. Ibid.

Stanford Beats the Odds, Ohio State

Stanford 27, Ohio State 17 • January 1, 1971

Ohio State seemed to have everything going for it entering its Rose Bowl game against Stanford. The Buckeyes, who had lost just once in the past three seasons, were 9-0, loaded with National Football League prospects and had a devastating running attack.

Stanford was 8-3 and had lost its final two regular-season games to Air Force and Cal.

But Stanford had Jim Plunkett, a senior quarterback capable of overcoming the longest of odds.

Raised by two blind parents in Northern California, Plunkett learned early that effort and belief in one's own ability are powerful tools in the face of adversity.

He possessed maturity beyond his years and had the special gift of being able to raise the level of performance of those around him.

Stanford needed someone such as Plunkett to rally around because this was a team that couldn't just step on the field and win by talent alone. "We felt we could beat anybody, but we had to play our best football," said Plunkett in 1991.

Stanford saved its best for the Buckeyes, relying on the passing of Plunkett and a hustling defense to upset Ohio State, 27–17, before 103,839 fans in Pasadena, California.

Two plays were crucial to Stanford's victory. On fourth and one from the Stanford 20 early in the fourth quarter, Ohio State fullback John Brockington was stopped short of a first down. The Buckeyes had marched 74 yards and were threatening to extend their 17–13 lead. Suddenly, momentum changed.

Stanford then drove 80 yards to take a 20–17 lead. The big play of the drive was a 35-yard pass from Plunkett to tight end Bob Moore, who leaped between two defenders to grab the ball on the two-yard line. It came on a third-and-sixteen situation, with Plunkett scrambling out of the pocket before spotting Moore downfield.

"When Jim was pressured and flushed right, my rule at that point was to go for the flag," Moore said. "Their safety man [Mike Sensibaugh] was right with me, but Jim threw a perfect pass."[1]

Plunkett finished with 20 completions in 30 attempts for 265 yards and one touchdown. He no doubt benefited from the fact Ohio State rarely had faced a pro-style passing attack similar to Stanford's. Besides Plunkett, Stanford's defense also performed admirably at key times.

Ohio State gained 364 yards rushing as quarterback Rex Kern and Brockington accumulated impressive statistics. Kern rushed for 129 yards in 20 carries and Brockington gained 101 yards in 21 carries. But the Buckeyes were halted in short-yardage situations and could do little in the decisive fourth quarter.

Stanford quarterback Jim Plunkett. (Photo courtesy of Stanford Sports Information Department.)

112   Stanford 27, Ohio State 17 (1971)

Forced to pass in the fourth quarter, Kern struggled. He finished 4 of 13 for 40 yards. His fourth-quarter interception set up Stanford's final touchdown, a ten-yard pass from Plunkett to Randy Vataha.

Afterward, Ohio State Coach Woody Hayes said, "We got beat by a better team. It was a game on which either team could have won it until we got stopped on their 20 and then they threw that 'mad-dog' pass to the two-yard line that set up their go-ahead touchdown."[2]

There were several important factors in the game's two decisive plays.

On Ohio State's fourth-down play, Stanford cornerback Charles McCloud aggressively raced up and turned Brockington inside, where teammates Jack Schultz, Ron Kadziel and Dave Tipton converged to halt the powerful Brockington. On Moore's reception, Ohio State gave Plunkett too much time to throw, rushing only three men. When Plunkett moved out of the pocket, Moore broke off his short pattern and sprinted toward the end zone.

But most important was Stanford's fearless attitude. Coach John Ralston made sure the players were not intimidated by their opposition. So what if Stanford had lost its final two regular-season games? "Stanford usually plays well against the good teams but not so well against teams not considered very good," Plunkett said. "It's just our history."

Ohio State was no ordinary team. Stanford players knew they would need to play above and beyond their normal levels.

"I think if we could have played them ten times, they probably would have won nine of them," Plunkett said. "But not that particular day. It is a situation where the little guy just sucks it up and plays his heart out. That's what our guys did. We had people on defense who just did a tremendous job, hustled and came up with big plays. On offense, although we were up against a bigger, stronger defensive unit, our guys played tougher."

Among the Stanford heroes was center John Sande, who went up against Ohio State's Jim Stillwagon, regarded as the season's top interior lineman in college football. Sande's effective blocking enabled Plunkett to break loose on quarterback draw plays that surprised the Buckeyes.

Also, strong safety Schultz helped contain Ohio State's option attack in the second half and came up with a fourth-quarter interception of Kern that iced the game.

Stanford opened a 10–0 lead in the first quarter before Ohio State rallied to go on top, 14–10 at halftime. An exchange of field goals in the third quarter set the stage for Stanford's overwhelming fourth-quarter performance.

For the 6-foot-3 Plunkett, the victory sustained his beliefs about what it requires to be successful.

"I couldn't have been prouder about a group of guys than I was that particular day," said Plunkett. "I played with a lot of people who might have been on the slight side as far as physical ability, but you couldn't replace what they had inside."

Postscript: The loss cost Ohio State the national championship. Texas and Nebraska ended up co-national champions. Ohio State finished No. 5 and Stanford No. 8 in the Associated Press rankings. Plunkett, who in 1970 became the first Stanford player to win the Heisman Trophy, was the first player taken in the 1971 National Football League draft when he was picked by the New England Patriots.

Plunkett played 17 years in the NFL with the Patriots, San Francisco 49ers and Oakland/Los Angeles Raiders. He was the most valuable player when the Oakland Raiders defeated the Philadelphia Eagles, 27–10, in the 1981 Super Bowl and was the quarterback when the Los Angeles Raiders routed the Washington Redskins, 38–9, in the 1984 Super Bowl.

Ohio State had four players taken in the first round of the 1971 NFL draft: running backs Brockington (Green Bay Packers) and Leo Hayden (Minnesota Vikings) and defensive backs Jack Tatum (Oakland Raiders) and Bill Anderson (San Francisco 49ers).

Brockington earned NFL rookie-of-the-year honors and was the first running back to rush for 1,000 yards in each of his first three seasons. Kern was a tenth-round pick of the Baltimore Colts and played for nine seasons as a defensive back. Lineman Stillwagon won college football's Rockne, Lombardi and Outland awards.

References

1. *Los Angeles Times,* 2 January 1971.
2. Ibid.

Nebraska Lives Up
to No. 1 Billing

Nebraska 35, Oklahoma 31 • November 25, 1971

Nebraska's road to repeating as national champion was paved with a formidable late-season obstacle: Oklahoma.

The Cornhuskers were No. 1 and the Sooners No. 2 when they met on Thanksgiving Day. When it was over, Nebraska remained No. 1. The Cornhuskers rallied for a 35–31 victory to nail down the Big Eight championship before 63,385 fans at Owen Stadium in Norman, Oklahoma.

Nebraska opened leads of 14-3 and 28-17, but Oklahoma came back behind quarterback Jack Mildren to go on top, 31-28, with 7:10 remaining.

Finally, Nebraska's chance for a national title and unbeaten season came down to a final drive, and the Cornhuskers had the nation's best quarterback to guide them in Jerry Tagge. He moved Nebraska 74 yards in 12 plays, with workhorse tailback Jeff Kinney ramming in from the two for his fourth touchdown of the day with 1:38 remaining to give Nebraska the victory.

How well was the game played? Only one penalty was called and the teams combined for 829 yards in total offense.

The one individual play long talked about was the scintillating punt return by Nebraska's Johnny Rodgers in the game's opening 3½ minutes. He went 72 yards for a touchdown, twisting and sprinting past the best and fastest defenders. He was hit almost immediately after catching the punt, recovered and took off. Rodgers finished with only one touchdown — compared to Kinney's four — but this one provided the Cornhuskers (11-0) with an early cushion.

Most surprising to Nebraska Coach Bob Devaney was the difficulty that his team's defense experienced in trying to stop the Oklahoma wishbone. Sure, the Sooners were averaging a staggering 481 yards per game rushing, but Nebraska's defense was second to none. Middle guard Rich Glover, tackle Larry Jacobson and linebacker Willie Harper had the ability to shut down just about any team.

So imagine Devaney's horror as Mildren's wishbone wizardry

racked up big yardage. The Sooners (9-1) totaled 467 yards in total offense against the best defense in the nation and were up by three points when Nebraska took over on its final possession.

"We got the ball and we knew we'd probably not have another shot because the way the game was going," Devaney said 20 years later.

Tagge took charge and Kinney became a one-man wrecking crew, running again and again up the middle for tough yardage. Kinney was the type of runner who drew defenders to him, then carried them along. Tagge would call a play in the huddle, walk up to the line and then call an audible, sending Kenney plowing ahead with the ball.

Nebraska faced a third-and-eight situation at the Oklahoma 46 with under five minutes left. Tagge was no scrambler, but as he dropped back to pass, Oklahoma was in position to sack him and probably win the game. He ran for his life and just before going down, he drilled the ball to Rodgers between two linebackers. Rodgers caught the low pass as he went to his knees for a first down at the 35.

Soon, it was up to Kinney again, running out of the powerful I-formation. He carried for thirteen yards, then seven yards on an inside reverse. Then four straight power runs by Kinney got the ball into the end zone, the last one behind tackle Daryl White. Kinney finished with 174 yards in 31 carries.

Crucial to the Cornhuskers' victory was denying the big play to Oklahoma's versatile halfback, Greg Pruitt, who was averaging 9.5 yards per carry. He was limited to 53 yards in 10 carries.

"They always had two guys outside and they did a great job of reading the blocks of the backs," said Pruitt afterward.[1]

Looking back, Devaney said, "It was the best team I ever coached and the only close game we had, and we played some pretty good football teams.

"I had a bunch of good athletes. It was a great team to coach, a team you didn't have to drive hard."

If not for Rodgers, Tagge and Kinney, Mildren would have been the most talked-about player in the game. Running the wishbone offense that Coach Chuck Fairbanks had installed the same year, Mildren was brilliant. He ran for 130 yards in 31 carries and scored two touchdowns. He also passed for 137 yards and two touchdowns.

Asked what he remembered most about the titanic clash of undefeated teams, Devaney said in 1991, "My best memory is when they shot the gun off at the end of the game and we were still ahead."

Nebraska Coach Bob Devaney.

Postscript: Nebraska defeated previously undefeated and second-ranked Alabama, 38–6, to finish the season 13-0 and win its second straight national title. The Cornhuskers ended the season with a 32-game undefeated streak. Oklahoma defeated Auburn and Heisman Trophy winner Pat Sullivan, 40–22, in the Sugar Bowl to finish 11-1 and ranked second by the Associated Press.

Jacobson won the Outland Trophy for being the nation's outstanding lineman. Tagge threw for 2,019 yards and 17 touchdowns. He was drafted in the first round by the Green Bay Packers. Rodgers ended up with 17 touchdowns and Kinney had 16. Kinney was a first-round draft pick of the Kansas City Chiefs. Rodgers won the Heisman Trophy in 1972.

Mildren set an NCAA rushing record for quarterbacks by averaging 103.6 yards a game. Pruitt finished third in the nation in rushing with 1,665 yards and 17 touchdowns.

Oklahoma gained 6,232 yards in total offense, 980 more than any other major college team. The Sooners set a record by averaging an NCAA-record 472.4 yards per game on the ground.

Reference

1. *Sports Illustrated*, 6 December 1971.

Stanford Repeats Rose Bowl Upset

Stanford 13, Michigan 12 • January 1, 1972

It had become fashionable to dismiss Stanford's football team as a bunch of intellectuals who had no business playing unbeaten Michigan in the Rose Bowl.

Sure, Stanford upset Ohio State in the 1971 Rose Bowl, but Heisman Trophy winner Jim Plunkett was the quarterback. Plunkett had been replaced by Don Bunce, a fifth-year senior more inclined to pursue a medical career than one in professional football. Bunce personified a team that was lean and not so mean.

As Stanford linebacker Jeff Siemon said, "If you saw these guys in street clothes, you'd never believe they're football players. It's such an incredible mixture of personalities and interests."[1]

So imagine the joy these players felt after Rod Garcia, the Stanford kicker who missed five field goals against San Jose State, made a 31-yard field goal with 12 seconds left to give Stanford a 13–12 victory over previously undefeated Michigan before 103,154 fans in Pasadena, California.

"It was an upset by everybody's standards, but I remember walking off the field thinking, 'What's everybody so excited about?'" Bunce said in 1991. "It was like, 'This was my dream for my entire life,' and I had

Stanford quarterback Don Bunce. (Photo courtesy of Stanford Sports Information Department.)

replayed this game over many times in my mind. I wasn't sure how it was going to happen, but I knew it had to be."

Five years earlier, Bunce had the misfortune to arrive at Stanford at the same time as Plunkett. "When I came to Stanford, I had never heard of Jim Plunkett, nor had most people," he said. "In fact, they experimented with him playing defensive end."

Plunkett eventually won the quarterback job, and Bunce ended up redshirting in 1970, the season Stanford won the Rose Bowl and Plunkett the Heisman Trophy. So now Bunce had his chance to enjoy the Rose Bowl experience and he wasn't about to let it pass without a successful ending.

Stanford was behind, 12–10, with 1:48 left when Bunce walked into the huddle knowing the game was on the line.

"I would usually say something to the team," Bunce said. "I looked up into the huddle and everybody's attention was just there. They were so focused and the sense of purpose so strong that I realized words were totally inappropriate."

Instead, he let his actions do the talking. He drove his team 64 yards in 8 plays. He completed passes of 13 yards to tight end Bill Scott, 16 yards to flanker John Winesberry, 11 yards to split end Miles Moore, 14 yards to fullback Reggie Sanderson and 12 to Winesberry. Finally, it was time to Garcia to come onto the field.

Garcia's teammates remembered the San Jose State game seven weeks before, when he had missed five field goals. Stanford Coach John Ralston had talked with Garcia before each kick that day. This time, he kept his thoughts to himself and Garcia delivered.

"Nobody can say I coach misses anymore," Ralston said.[2]

"I said a little prayer for him" stated Stanford defensive tackle Pete Lazetich. "He's our garbanzo bean — that's what we call him. After he made that kick, after we won the game, I cried like a baby, I really did."[3]

Yes, Stanford really did want to win, although sometimes that might not have been the impression given to outsiders.

"We were sort of delighted we were underdogs and were a loose group of guys who had a different philosophy about football," Bunce said. "In fact, people don't know this, but we actually boycotted practice [for the Rose Bowl game] because it was our feeling if we had a good season, playing in the Rose Bowl was a reward.

"We wanted to enjoy Disneyland and go to all the things planned for us. We decided we weren't going to go out until these demands were met. We sort of had a good time. I think it was a misinterpretation by our coach that we just wanted to have fun and lose sight of the importance of the game, but what we were telling him is that we wanted more say in some of the decisions being made."

Despite the threats, Stanford players did show up for practice and then showed up Michigan.

Michigan, a 10½-point favorite, had an offense that tried to run the ball again and again. It was Michigan Coach Bo Schembechler at his conservative best. Quarterback Tom Slade entered the game having attempted just 53 passes all season and he ended up completing 3 of 10 for 26 yards.

Michigan (11-1) held a 3–0 halftime lead, then Stanford tied it, 3–3, in the third quarter on Garcia's 42-yard field goal. Michigan regained the lead, 10–3, on the fourth play of the fourth quarter when Fritz Seyferth scored from the one. Then Stanford (9-3) tied it, 10–10, with running back Jackie Smith running 33 yards with a fake punt, then sprinting 24 yards for a touchdown with 8:31 left.

Michigan seemingly took the lead for good on a safety with 3:18 left to play. A 46-yard field-goal attempt by Michigan's Dana Coin was short, and Stanford's Jim Ferguson had tried to run it out of the end zone. He got to the six, then went backwards and was tackled by Ed Shuttlesworth in the end zone.

But Bunce was finding success with the pass, as Michigan had trouble applying pressure on him and kept leaving Stanford running backs open out of the backfield. Bunce completed 24 of 44 passes for 290 yards.

"Bo was so predictable that he had a middle linebacker basically covering two backs, so we ran both backs right at the middle linebacker, who had to take one or the other," Bunce said. "We kept throwing these short dump-off passes to our backs. The middle linebacker would cover one and I'd throw to the other."

Stanford's defense also contributed heavily, especially sophomore safety Randy Poltl, who had 14 tackles.

As for which of his two Rose Bowl victories felt sweeter, Ralston said, "The first time you win here, it's the greatest moment in your life. But this is a great thrill too. I guess maybe I can't explain it, but it's wonderful."[4]

Postscript: Michigan finished sixth in the rankings by the Associated Press; Stanford was ranked tenth.

Bunce played a year with the British Columbia Lions of the Canadian Football League, then retired from football to attend medical school. He became an orthopedic surgeon, returning to Stanford to serve as the team doctor. Stanford had two players selected in the first round of the National Football League draft, with lineman Greg Sampson going to the Houston Oilers and Siemon going to the Minnesota Vikings.

Ralston resigned at the end of the season to become head coach of the Denver Broncos. He was 55-36-3 in nine years at Stanford.

References

1. *Los Angeles Times,* 2 January 1972.
2. Ibid.
3. Ibid.
4. Ibid.

UCLA's Wishbone Cracks No. 1 Nebraska

UCLA 20, Nebraska 17 • September 9, 1972

As ambushes go, UCLA pulled off a king-sized one in its season opener. The victim was two-time defending national champion Nebraska.

Before the game, all signs pointed to a Nebraska blowout. UCLA, a 15-point underdog, was 2-7-1 the previous season. Only one defensive starter was back.

The Bruins were unveiling the run-oriented wishbone offense directed by quarterback Mark Harmon. Nebraska, under veteran Coach Bob Devaney, was ranked the preseason No. 1 team in the nation. The Cornhuskers had a 32-game unbeaten streak and possessed three legitimate Heisman Trophy candidates in slotback Johnny Rodgers, defensive end Willie Harper and middle guard Rich Glover.

Surprise—UCLA won, 20–17, on Efren Herrera's 30-yard field goal with 22 seconds left before 67,702 fans at the Los Angeles Memorial Coliseum.

Nebraska turned the ball over five times, helping UCLA score 17 of its 20 points.

At the same time, UCLA's high-risk wishbone offense worked better than expected under the guidance of Harmon, a junior college transfer who showed superb poise and leadership for someone playing in his first major college game.

UCLA led 10–0, then Nebraska tied it at 10 by halftime. UCLA led 17–10, then Nebraska tied it again. Finally, it was up to Harmon to give UCLA a chance to win on its final possession.

He moved the Bruins downfield on a 57-yard drive, making sure there were no fumbles or interceptions to ruin the upset opportunity. It came down to a decisive moment: third and eleven at the Nebraska 33. For UCLA, this was no time to be conservative. Harmon completed a 13-yard pass to tight end Jack Lassner down the middle for a first down. Soon, Herrera came on to kick the winning field goal.

Devaney was concerned before the game about how his team would respond under sophomore quarterback David Humm, who was replacing Jerry Tagge, a first-round selection of the Green Bay Packers. Humm showed his inexperience, throwing two interceptions.

"Our players knew UCLA was going to be ready to play," said Devaney afterward. "It was not a matter of overconfidence at all. When we went out in the second half tied at 10, I thought we were going to win. But we never really managed to take the momentum away from them."[1]

The unsung Bruins' defense may have been loaded with inexperienced juniors and sophomores, but there was plenty of talent, led by cornerback Jim Allen, who had two interceptions, and linebacker Fred McNeil. The Bruins limited Rodgers to 43 yards rushing and three receptions for 63 yards.

"I didn't know how good our defense would be," said UCLA Coach Pepper Rodgers. "We're not pros, all sophomores and juniors, but I knew we had speed and character and attitude. Emotion was a big factor for us. We were ready to play."[2]

The game also marked the much-anticipated varsity debut together of running backs Kermit Johnson and James McAlister. The two had led Blair High School in Pasadena, California, to a sectional championship and were highly recruited. McAlister, though, had to sit out his sophomore season because of questions regarding his Scholastic Aptitude Test scores.

UCLA quarterback Mark Harmon. (Photo courtesy of UCLA Sports Information Department.)

124   UCLA 20, Nebraska 17 (1972)

UCLA fans decided it was worth the wait. McAlister rushed for 90 yards in 18 carries, displaying power and speed. Johnson picked up 35 yards in 12 carries.

As for Harmon, the son of former Michigan Heisman Trophy winner Tom Harmon, he rushed for 77 yards and completed four of eight passes for 65 yards and a touchdown, a 46-yard second-quarter toss to Brad Lyman.

Coach Rodgers had made the decision to switch to the wishbone, and UCLA offensive coordinator Homer Smith was given the task of installing it.

"Mark had been so eager about learning the wishbone and had worked so hard that I was really gratified he did so well after all the investment he had made," Smith said in 1991.

"I gained a lot of respect for Mark," added Johnson in 1991. "If you look back, Mark had to take some helluva shots for that wishbone to work right.

"He ran that wishbone just like no other quarterback has run it. There were times he took shots just to draw defenders to him to eliminate them and then pitched the ball."

Postscript: Nebraska routed Notre Dame, 40–6, in the Orange Bowl to finish 9-2-1 and was ranked fourth by the Associated Press. Johnny Rodgers won the Heisman Trophy and Glover won the Outland Trophy. Rodgers was drafted in the first round by the San Diego Chargers in 1973.

Devaney retired from coaching at the end of the 1972 season to become the school's athletic director. From 1962 to 1972, his teams went 101-20-2 and won two national titles and eight Big Eight championships.

UCLA finished 8-3 and was ranked 15th. Harmon left the football field in 1974 to become a successful actor. Johnson and McAlister each played in the National Football League. Johnson averaged 6.7 yards per carry during his three-year UCLA career, finishing with 2,495 yards and 25 touchdowns. McAlister gained 1,492 yards in his two seasons.

Allen and McNeil played against each other in the 1975 Super Bowl, with Allen on the Pittsburgh Steelers and McNeil with the Minnesota Vikings. Pepper Rodgers resigned after the 1973 season to become head coach at Georgia Tech, his alma mater. His three-year record at UCLA was 19-12-1.

References

1. *Los Angeles Times,* 10 September 1972.
2. Ibid.

USC's Davis Flashes into Spotlight

USC 45, Notre Dame 23 • December 2, 1972

Six touchdowns! Who would have expected it?

Only a few weeks earlier, Anthony Davis was just another non-starter for USC. But against Notre Dame, Davis emerged as one of the nation's most potent weapons, returning two kickoffs for touchdowns and scoring four other touchdowns in the Trojans' 45-23 conquest of Notre Dame before 75,243 fans at the Los Angeles Memorial Coliseum.

And all this from a sophomore.

After it was over, Notre Dame Coach Ara Parseghian could only bemoan his misfortune.

"The worst part about [Davis] is that I have to look at him the next couple of years," Parseghian said.[1]

Although the score was lopsided, Notre Dame was on the Trojans' heels late in the third quarter before being struck down by a 5-foot-9 lightening bolt in the person of Davis.

Davis had romped 97 yards on the opening kickoff to help catapult the Trojans to a 19-3 first-quarter lead. But his powerful and elusive scats were needed once again after sophomore quarterback Tom Clements had thrown his third touchdown pass to bring the Irish to within 25-23.

Notre Dame's ensuing kickoff went just out of bounds and the Irish were penalized five yards.

The next boot by Cliff Brown sailed high and deep to Davis, who caught the ball on the USC four-yard line, located an opening and wheeled to his right and into the clear. Davis streaked past safety Tim Rudnick on the sidelines near the Notre Dame 25-yard line en route to a 96-yard touchdown that summarily ended Notre Dame's comeback hopes.

USC running back Anthony Davis. (Photo courtesy of USC Sports Information Department.)

"I was trying to hold him up so I could get some help," Rudnick said. "But he made a quick move to the middle of the field and I went with it. Then he was back to the outside and was gone. No one could be any quicker."[2]

Davis also ran for touchdowns of eight, five, four and one yard, finishing with 99 yards in 22 carries and caught three passes for 51 yards.

USC Coach John McKay acknowledged Davis' sensational game, but noted that he benefited from being surrounded by considerable talent. "Anthony was playing on one of the greatest college football teams in the country," said McKay in 1991. "Our fullback was [future NFL player] Sam Cunningham. Anthony was a real good back, but he never got as good as I thought he'd get [after college]."

The victory was testimony to the Trojans' No. 1 national ranking. Notre Dame, at 8-1 entering the game, was considered a formidable opponent although critics had maligned the Irish's supposedly soft schedule.

USC 45, Notre Dame 23 (1972)   127

Still, Davis had no doubt that USC would prevail. And he even said so before the opening kickoff.

"Before the game, the locker room was real quiet," said Davis in 1990, "and everyone was nervous. I walked in and said, 'Hey, what's with everyone? We're going to beat them just like we beat everyone else.' What did I know about pressure and the game? I was just 18 years old."[3]

Interestingly, the Irish won the statistical battle, gaining the upper hand in yards, 360–320; first downs, 19–18; and total plays, 75–61. But Notre Dame failed to execute when it needed to most.

"We had the momentum [trailing 25–23] until that last kickoff return," Parseghian said. "We just made too many errors. Those two kickoff returns and fumbles, interceptions and pass interference calls are mistakes that you can't make against a good team."[4]

Davis built his seasonal rushing total to 1,034 yards and joined a select USC 1,000-yard club that included Morley Drury, Mike Garrett, O. J. Simpson and Clarence Davis.

Davis was revved up before the game but was more subdued after it was over.

"I wanted to do well," he said, "because our seniors, especially the guys on our offensive team, had been so frustrated for two years. They had never been to the Rose Bowl or won a national championship."[5]

USC needed a strong effort from Davis because quarterback Mike Rae had difficulty finding open receivers against a defense that laid back in coverage. While Clements completed 14 of 24 passes for 199 yards, Rae threw for only 150 yards, completing 10 of 20.

Although USC's offense was kept in check somewhat, Davis wasn't. His one-yard touchdown run in the first quarter gave the Trojans a 13–3 lead and his third touchdown of the quarter, a five-yard sweep, lifted USC into a 19–3 lead.

Davis scored on a four-yard run early in the third quarter to hike the Trojans' lead to 25–10, but his biggest contribution came on his second touchdown return.

Asked whether he should have ordered a squib kick instead of giving Davis another chance for a long runback in the third quarter, Parseghian said, "We wanted to pin them down in their own territory. We didn't want them to get the ball around the 25- and 40-yard line. We have a lot of young people on our kickoff coverage.

"We use younger people because they're aggressive at getting downfield. They've done a fine job, but they don't always come up against a guy like Davis."[6]

Postscript: Cunningham scored four touchdowns to lead USC to a 42–17 victory over Ohio State in the Rose Bowl as the Trojans nailed down the No. 1 ranking with a 12-0 record.

Notre Dame ended the season with its second consecutive loss, dropping a 40–6 decision to Nebraska in the Orange Bowl to finish at 8-3. The Fighting Irish were ranked 14th by the Associated Press.

Davis enjoyed a brilliant three-year career at USC, leading the Trojans in rushing all three years. He gained 1,191 yards as a sophomore, 1,112 as a junior and 1,421 as a senior in the Heisman Trophy balloting behind Ohio State's Archie Griffin.

Davis rushed for 1,200 yards in his rookie season for the Southern California Sun of the World Football League, but failed to distinguish himself thereafter although he competed in four professional football leagues — World, Canadian, National and United States.

References

1. *Los Angeles Times,* 3 December 1972.
2. Ibid.
3. *Los Angeles Times,* 14 July 1990.
4. *Los Angeles Times,* 3 December 1972.
5. Ibid.
6. Ibid.

Michigan Fit to Be Tied

Ohio State 10, Michigan 10 • November 24, 1973

Finesse took a backseat when Ohio State and Michigan slugged it out in a Big Ten showdown in Ann Arbor, Michigan.

The hitting was vicious and the intensity was at a feverish pitch. A berth in the Rose Bowl, the conference championship and perhaps the national championship were at stake.

There were 105,223 people in attendance, setting a record for the largest crowd to watch a regular-season college game. Ohio State was 9-0 and ranked No. 1. Michigan was 10-0 and ranked No. 4. Ohio State had recorded four shutouts, Michigan three.

Ohio State opened a 10–0 halftime lead. Michigan scored 10 points in the fourth quarter to tie the score, but the Wolverines missed on two long field-goal attempts in the final two minutes and the game ended in a 10–10 tie.

"It was without question the toughest Ohio State–Michigan game," Ohio State's Archie Griffin, one of the game's key players, recalled 18 years later. "It was knock 'em, rock 'em, sock 'em. We stuck completely to the running game. Our quarterback the week before had injured his hand and couldn't pass. They had an outstanding defense and adjusted."

As if the players and game weren't enough of an attraction, the coaches added to the entertainment. Ohio State's Woody Hayes and Michigan's Bo Schembechler acted like emotional generals commanding an army.

"I would imagine Bo wanted to beat Woody just as much as Woody wanted to beat Bo," Griffin said.

The coaches shared another characteristic. Both were not particularly fond of the pass. "If you pass, three things can happen and two of them are bad," Griffin said about the Hayes' philosophy.

Schembechler, though, had a quarterback in Dennis Franklin who had a good arm and wasn't afraid to use it.

So the game featured two offenses intent on wearing down the opposing defenses. Ohio State tried 49 consecutive running plays, a challenge for the best of defenses. Michigan stopped the Buckeyes throughout the second half. Griffin, a sophomore, left the game in the fourth quarter with a leg injury after rushing for 163 yards in 30 carries.

Griffin's running set up a 31-yard field goal by Blair Conway and a 5-yard touchdown run by Pete Johnson, both in the second quarter, that gave Ohio State a 10–0 halftime lead.

Michigan's defense began to take control late in the third quarter. The Wolverines took over the momentum after they stopped Ohio State quarterback Cornelius Greene on fourth and two from the Wolverine 34.

Suddenly, Michigan began to move the ball behind fullback Ed Shuttlesworth, who finished with 116 yards in 27 carries. Shuttlesworth carried on 8 of 11 plays to enable Mike Lantry to kick a 30-yard field

Ohio State running back Archie Griffin. (Photo courtesy of Ohio State Sports Information Department.)

goal early in the fourth quarter. Then Michigan tied the score, 10–10, on a 49-yard drive that featured a 27-yard pass from Franklin to Paul Seal. Franklin scored the tying touchdown on a 10-yard run on fourth down.

What crippled Michigan most of all was a broken collarbone suffered by Franklin just as he was guiding the Wolverines to a potential game-winning score.

Michigan was on the Ohio State 48 when Franklin was hurt. Backup Larry Cipa came in with 2:25 left, and Schembechler gave precise orders not to pass. After three running plays, Lantry barely missed a 58-yard field-goal attempt.

Ohio State then tried to mount a drive by passing. That was a mistake. Jon Drake intercepted a pass by backup quarterback Greg Hare and returned the ball to the 33 with 52 seconds remaining.

Again, Schembechler played it safe. With no time-outs and his first-string quarterback injured, the Wolverines got off a six-yard run and an incompleted pass before trying a field goal on third down. Lantry missed from 44 yards, leaving Ohio State and Michigan tied for the Big Ten championship.

Schembechler defended his play-calling afterward. "We didn't settle for a tie," he said. "We gambled in our own territory and did everything we could to win."[1]

Both teams wanted to win in the worst way. "Michigan was a season in itself," Griffin said. "That was a game you set out to win in the spring. A lot of the time in the spring was set out preparing for Michigan."

Postscript: One day later, the Big Ten athletic directors voted, 6–4, to send Ohio State to the Rose Bowl, provoking an irate Schembechler to say, "I'm very bitter. It's a tragic thing for Big Ten football."[2] Michigan thought it would get to go because Ohio State had gone the previous year. But the athletic directors were influenced by Franklin's injury, believing a weakened Michigan team might find it difficult to end the Big Ten's four-game losing streak in the Rose Bowl.

Ohio State made the athletic directors look smart when it beat USC, 42–21, in the Rose Bowl. The Buckeyes ended up 10-0-1 and ranked No. 2 behind Notre Dame (11-0) in the Associated Press poll. Michigan (10-0-1) was ranked No. 6. Griffin ended the season with 1,428 yards rushing. He went on to become the first two-time Heisman Trophy winner, picking up the award his junior and senior seasons. He finished with 5,177 yards rushing in his career and helped Ohio State secure at least a share of the Big Ten championship in each of his four years at the school.

Ohio State tackle John Hicks won the Outland and Lombardi awards as the nation's top lineman in 1973. Hicks finished second in the Heisman Trophy voting with 524 points. Penn State running back John Cappelletti was first with 1,057 points. Hayes and Schembechler faced each other ten times as coaches, with Schembechler holding a 5-4-1 advantage.

References

1. *Los Angeles Times,* 25 November 1973.
2. Ibid.

Parseghian Makes the Winning Call

Notre Dame 24, Alabama 23 • December 31, 1973

This time Notre Dame Coach Ara Parseghian gambled. And this time there would be no second-guessing as the Fighting Irish held off Alabama, 24–23, in the Sugar Bowl.

With less than three minutes remaining, the third-ranked Fighting Irish were stuck on their three-yard line, pinned down by a 69-yard punt. It was third down and eight yards to go, with Notre Dame clinging to a one-point lead over top-ranked Alabama.

The decision at hand was whether to run the ball, then punt and hope the Fighting Irish defense could prevent a game-winning field goal, or take a chance and go for the first down with a risky pass play.

Parseghian had been widely critcized in a 1966 game between the top-ranked Fighting Irish and second-ranked Michigan State for sitting on the ball in the final minute and settling for a 10–10 tie. But this time Parseghian decided to gamble.

Notre Dame lined up in run formation with two tight ends and a power-I backfield. Junior quarterback Tom Clements made a play-action fake and threw a 35-yard pass to tight end Robin Weber for the first down. Notre Dame then ran out the clock to secure the victory before a record crowd of 85,161 at Tulane Stadium in New Orleans.

"That's probably the most memorable play in my college career," Clements said 18 years later. "It was a great call."

"I knew damn well we weren't going to get the ball out beyond the 35 with a punt and they're immediately in field-goal range and we get beat," said Parseghian in 1991. "I thought it was a risky pass, but what

Notre Dame Coach Ara Parseghian. (Photo courtesy of Notre Dame Sports Information Department.)

really bothered me more and I told Tom, 'Don't try to run the ball' because he's such a good runner I didn't want to get him trapped and lose the game on a safety.

"We had designed the play to throw to Dave Casper. We were trying to clear out the defensive right halfback. Weber was supposed to drive out the right halfback and Casper was to cross over and be the principal receiver.

"The Alabama kid blows the assignment, lets Weber run right past him and Casper is running right into the coverage of the guy who made the mistake. Tom lofted the ball to Weber, who had caught one pass all year. My heart jumped into my mouth when I saw him juggle the ball. He damn near dropped it."

Notre Dame improved to 11-0, its first perfect record since 1949.

"There was a lot on the line," Parseghian said. "It was the first time

Notre Dame and Alabama had ever played. It was the first time [Alabama Coach] Bear Bryant and I had ever competed against each other. We both had undefeated teams and Bear claimed it was the best he ever had. It was the Baptists vs. the Catholics."

To no one's surprise, the game was every bit a thriller. The lead changed hands six times, the last coming when Notre Dame's Bob Thomas made a 19-yard field goal with 4:26 remaining.

The winning, 11-play, 79-yard drive featured a 30-yard pass from Clements to Casper. Clements breathed a sigh of relief when the 240-pound Casper grabbed the ball between two Alabama defenders.

"The ball slipped out of my hands and sort of hung up there for a while, but Casper came up with it," Clements said.

The game went back and forth. Notre Dame led, 6-0, on a six-yard touchdown run by Wayne Bullock. Alabama went up, 7-6, in the second quarter on Randy Billingsley's six-yard touchdown run. Then Notre Dame's Al Hunter returned a kickoff 93 yards for a touchdown and a 14-7 Irish lead. Alabama picked up a 39-yard field goal by Bill Davis, and the half ended with Notre Dame on top, 14-10.

Alabama (11-1) went 93 yards to start the second half, getting a five-yard touchdown run from Wilbur Jackson to take a 17-14 lead. Later in the third quarter, Notre Dame linebacker Drew Mahalic recovered a fumble in midair at the Alabama 12. Eric Penick ran 12 yards for the score and a 21-17 Irish lead.

Early in the fourth quarter, Alabama regained the lead on a trick play. Second-string quarterback Richard Todd handed the ball to halfback Mike Stock, who threw a pass back to Todd for a 25-yard touchdown.

But Clements would soon rescue the Irish, as he had done several times during the season. In fact, one reason Parseghian elected to throw on the decisive play of the game deep in Notre Dame territory was his complete confidence in Clements.

"He was probably the coolest quarterback under pressure that I ever had," Parseghian said. "I used to say, 'Third and short, fourth and goal, and any kind of critical play, you never saw him get a lump in his throat.' He was a guy in the huddle who demanded respect not by being a chatterbox or a holler guy, just by radiating confidence in the other guys."

Clements finished with 7 completions in 12 attempts for 169 yards. He also rushed for 74 yards in 15 carries. Jackson led Alabama's rushing

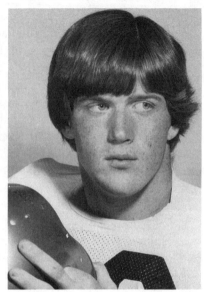

Left: Notre Dame quarterback Tom Clements. Right: Notre Dame tight end Dave Casper.

game with 62 yards in 11 carries. Alabama quarterback Gary Rutledge completed 7 of 12 passes for 88 yards.

Postscript: Notre Dame won its first national title since 1966. Clements played 13 years in the Canadian Football League, winning Grey Cups with Ottawa in 1976 and Winnipeg in 1984. He attended Notre Dame Law School during the off-season, graduated in 1986 and became an attorney in Chicago.

Casper became a star receiver for the Oakland Raiders. Parseghian coached Notre Dame for 11 years, resigning at the end of the 1974 season because of health reasons. He won three national championships and had a record of 95-17-4.

Alabama, ranked fourth by the Associated Press, failed to win a bowl game for the seventh consecutive time. Bryant coached for 38 years, winning more games than any other coach until the record was broken by Grambling's Eddie Robinson. Bryant was 323-85-17 (.780). He coached at Alabama from 1958–82.

USC Scores Final 55 Points in Huge Reversal

USC 55, Notre Dame 24 • November 30, 1974

It's rare that a team all but wraps up a victory before halftime, but Notre Dame appeared to do just that against USC at the Los Angeles Memorial Coliseum.

The fifth-ranked Fighting Irish bolted to a 24–0 lead with less than a minute remaining in the first half as 83,552 fans watched in disbelief, perhaps wondering if Notre Dame would duplicate its 51–0 blitz of the Trojans eight years earlier.

Two of USC's top players admitted in 1990 that they were less than optimistic facing such a large deficit.

"We just wanted to make the game respectable," tailback Anthony Davis said.

"Notre Dame had the No. 1–rated defense in the country," quarterback Pat Haden said. "It was not a great prospect to come back."

But come back USC did. The sixth-ranked Trojans scored the final 55 points en route to a 55–24 victory in one of the most remarkable reversals in college football history. USC outscored Notre Dame, 35–0, in the third quarter as Davis and Haden shrugged off lackluster starts to ignite the Trojans. Davis finished with four touchdowns and Haden tied a school record by throwing for four.

Scores of USC supporters streamed toward the exits after Notre Dame's Mark McLane scored from nine yards out with 53 seconds remaining in the first half to lift the Fighting Irish to their 24-point lead. But many returned from the parking lots after hearing the crowd roar when Haden tossed a seven-yard swing pass to Davis for a touchdown with ten seconds remaining in the half to bring the Trojans within 24–6.

Davis and Haden said the turning point came on the second-half kickoff. Davis had scored a remarkable six touchdowns against Notre Dame two years earlier—two on kickoff returns—but Notre Dame tempted fate and kicked it long against the Trojans.

Davis was waiting two yards deep in his end zone.

The 5-foot-9 Davis streaked to his left, broke a tackle and headed for the sideline. Mosi Tatupu and Mario Celotto delivered key blocks to spring Davis and then the Trojan senior outraced Ted Burgmeier to the end zone.

Although Haden was stopped on his run for the two-point conversion, the Trojans were now within, 24–12, and there would be no stopping them.

"People don't remember that no one was kicking off [deep] to our team," Davis said. "And it was the first end-over-end kick I got from Notre Dame since 1972.

"In the kickoff return huddle, I looked at everyone and said, 'If we're going to lose in the Coliseum, we'll go down fighting. Just block one guy and I'll get us field position or I'll bring it all the way back.'"

At halftime, USC Coach John McKay stressed the importance of scoring the first time the Trojans had the ball. "Coach McKay told us to get the second-half kickoff and go out and score," Haden said. "Anthony Davis took it literally."

The Trojans were just getting started.

"A real key play was Anthony returning the kickoff 102 yards," Haden said, "but on the ensuing kickoff, another real, real big play — and one that people don't remember — was that [USC's] Dave Lewis just clobbered their return man at the eight-yard line.

"It was a great special-teams play and bottled their team up. The momentum had really changed.... Angelenos have a tendency to be blasé, but there was tremendous electricity at the game. I had never experienced that before or since."

After the kickoff, Notre Dame quarterback Tom Clements was stymied by an aroused Trojan defense. USC then rattled off another four touchdowns before the quarter ended.

Davis' four-yard run with 8:37 left in the third quarter gave the Trojans their first lead at 27–24. As far as Davis was concerned, that was the game.

"I knew we had it won when we passed them," Davis said. "I knew then that they had lost it. They were a crumbling team. I could see it in their eyes. I've always made the quote, 'We turned into madmen.' And that's what we did. We turned into maniacs. And what made it altogether unbelievable is that we did it against the No. 1 defense in the country."

Wide receiver John McKay, the coach's son, caught two touchdown passes from Haden in the third quarter as the Trojans opened a 41–24 lead.

Then in the fourth quarter, Shelton Diggs scored on a 16-yard pass from Haden and Charles Phillips turned his third interception of a Clements pass into a 58-yard return for a touchdown with 13:16 remaining in the game. It was the Trojans' final touchdown.

Within a 17-minute span, USC had scored a shocking eight touchdowns, averaging a touchdown almost every two minutes.

USC's rapid scoring pace was even too much for the scoreboard, which went on the blink in the third quarter.

Haden finished with 11 completions in 17 attempts for 225 yards to help the Trojans improve to 9-1-1 and drop the Irish to 9-2. In the first half, Haden threw an interception and failed to convert a fourth-and-inches gamble from the USC 29 — both of which led to Notre Dame touchdowns.

But the USC senior completed eight of eight passes for 144 yards and four touchdowns within a 17-minute span to rally the Trojans. And in so doing, Haden eclipsed the school record of 30 touchdown passes in a career held by Jimmy Jones, throwing his 31st to McKay on a 44-yard pass on the last play of the third quarter.

Coach McKay, who previously had called Haden the best quarterback he had ever seen, took great satisfaction in Haden's performance. "I said it in the beginning, I said it in the middle, I say it now, Pat Haden is a great quarterback, an excellent runner and a great passer," McKay said afterward.[1]

Who could have predicted such an onslaught against the powerful Irish defense?

The Irish had allowed only eight touchdowns in their previous ten games — which USC matched in one day. But there was precedent for a Trojan comeback against the Irish. In 1964, the Trojans had trailed, 17–0, before rallying for a 20–17 victory.

Ten years later, the Trojans were set in motion by the emotion of Davis' kickoff return. "That was the key," said Davis, who rushed for 48 yards in 18 carries and had three receptions for 37 yards. "It turned the momentum and kicked off Haden and everyone else."

Postscript: Haden led USC to an 18–17 comeback victory over Ohio State in the Rose Bowl game, throwing a 38-yard touchdown pass to McKay with 2:03 remaining, then connecting with Diggs for the two-point conversion. USC (10-1-1) finished as the No. 1–ranked team in United Press International's coaches poll and second behind Oklahoma in the Associated Press' writers poll.

Two weeks after Notre Dame's loss to USC, Ara Parseghian announced that he would resign as the Fighting Irish football coach at the end of the season. Then he guided Notre Dame to a 13–11 upset over previously undefeated Alabama in the Orange Bowl to end the Crimson Tide's hopes for a national championship. Notre Dame (10-2) finished No. 6 in AP's poll.

Reference

1. *Sports Illustrated*, 9 December 1974.

USC Shuns Tie, Overcomes Ohio State

USC 18, Ohio State 17 • January 1, 1975

USC Coach John McKay faced a big decision after the Trojans scored a late touchdown to close within a point of Ohio State in the Rose Bowl game. It wasn't, however, a difficult decision for him to make.

McKay passed up the extra-point kick and the almost certain tie to attempt a two-point conversion. The gamble paid off.

USC quarterback Pat Haden connected with a diving Shelton Diggs deep in the end zone to give the fourth-ranked Trojans an 18–17 victory over the second-ranked Buckeyes before 106,721 fans in Pasadena, California.

"We always go for the two points in a situation like that," said McKay afterward. "We didn't come to play for a tie. We were a fortunate team to win. They were unfortunate to lose."[1]

McKay often gambled in similar situations. And he usually came up empty. His 1961 team lost one-point decisions to Iowa and Pittsburgh because of gambles gone awry. And McKay eschewed a possible tie in the 1967 Rose Bowl game against Purdue, gambling for a two-point conversion but getting a 14–13 loss instead. But with a national title within reach, McKay knew this was no time to turn conservative.

"There were 106,000 people in the stands and no one knew who would win right until the end," McKay said. "I thought it was a great game between two great teams and in the end we had 18 points and they had 17."[2]

McKay said in 1991 he was confident that the Trojans would score the two-point conversion. "I felt we could make it seventy-five percent of the time," he said. "We weren't going to kick it. Even if I were only ten percent confident, I would have still gone for it.

"My philosophy is that once they put in the rule that you could go for two points, why play all that time and still be tied?" McKay added.

USC (10-1-1) scored its final touchdown on a four-minute drive engineered by Haden. Tailback Allen Carter, filling in for the injured Anthony Davis, and fullbacks Dave Farmer and Ricky Bell took turns running the ball, advancing the Trojans to the Buckeye 38. From there, Haden lofted an arching pass to his former Bishop Amat High School teammate and the coach's son, John McKay, who caught the touchdown pass in the corner of the end zone with 2:03 remaining.

It was the second touchdown pass of the game for Haden, who completed 12 of 22 passes for 181 yards. Early in the fourth quarter, Haden gave USC a 10-7 lead when he hit tight end Jim Obradovich for a nine-yard touchdown. Ohio State All-American cornerback Neal Colzie, who already had two interceptions, tried for his third, but arrived too late as Obradovich made the catch at the one and fell into the end zone.

The game matched two of the premier running backs in the country in Davis and Ohio State's Archie Griffin. But that much-anticipated duel fizzled. Davis was injured in the first half and did not play after halftime. And Griffin was held in check most of the day and fumbled away two Ohio State scoring drives inside the Trojan ten-yard line.

Davis gained 67 yards in 13 carries before injuring his leg and sternum. Carter, however, was outstanding as Davis' replacement, leading the Trojans' ground game on USC's two long fourth-quarter scoring drives.

Griffin, meanwhile, collected only 75 yards in 20 carries. Ohio State's junior quarterback, Cornelius Greene, baffled the Trojans with his elusive runs, rushing for 52 yards in addition to passing for 93 yards.

Greene, in fact, made a game bid to pull out the victory after USC had taken its 18-17 lead. He marched the Buckeyes (10-2) to the USC

45, but Tom Skladany, normally a punter, was short on his 62-yard field-goal attempt as the game ended.

Often cantankerous in defeat, Ohio State Coach Woody Hayes was mild this time. "We got beaten by a better team," Hayes said. "One point better."[3]

Postscript: USC jumped to No. 1 in United Press International's coaches poll and second behind Oklahoma in the Associated Press' writers poll. Ohio State fell to No. 4 in the AP poll.

McKay was USC's head coach for 16 years. When he left to become the head coach of the Tampa Bay Buccaneers after the 1975 season, his teams had won more games (127) than any other USC coach. His teams won four national titles: 1962, 1967, 1972 and 1974. McKay enjoyed far less success at Tampa Bay. In the Buccaneers' first season in 1976, Tampa Bay went winless in 14 games. Tampa Bay's losing streak hit 26 in 1977. McKay's Buccaneers, however, did win National Football Conference Central Division titles in 1979 (10-6) and in 1981 (9-7). McKay retired after the 1984 season. In nine seasons, McKay's Buccaneer teams went 44-88-1.

Davis placed second in the Heisman Trophy balloting, garnering 819 points to finish behind Griffin, who had 1,920.

Davis went on to enjoy a strong rookie season (1,200 yards rushing) for the Southern California Sun of the World Football League, but failed to distinguish himself thereafter although he did become the first player to compete in four professional football leagues — World, Canadian, National and United States.

The 5-foot-8¾ Griffin also won the Heisman Trophy his senior year, becoming the first two-time Heisman winner.

Griffin ended his collegiate career with 5,177 yards rushing. He gained at least 100 yards in 33 games. In Griffin's four years, Ohio State went 40-5-1 and won at least a share of four Big Ten championships.

Haden played quarterback for the Los Angeles Rams for six years, throwing for 9,296 yards from 1976–81.

References

1. Gene Brown, *The New York Times Scrapbook Encyclopedia of Sports History — The Complete Book of Football* (Indianapolis/New York: Bobbs-Merrill Company, Inc., 1980).
2. *Los Angeles Times*, 2 January 1975.
3. Ibid.

USC Outlasts
Notre Dame, Montana

USC 27, Notre Dame 25 • November 25, 1978

Not even the most ingenious roller-coaster ride could produce the rousing mood changes or improbable happenings that took place in the 50th meeting between USC and Notre Dame.

This is college football's most famous intersectional series, and no one doubted its special place in American sports history after USC pulled out a 27–25 victory on a 37-yard field goal with two seconds left before 84,256 fans at the Los Angeles Memorial Coliseum.

USC held a 24–6 lead at the outset of the fourth quarter. Notre Dame quarterback Joe Montana had fumbled away the ball on USC's one-yard line the previous quarter. The Fighting Irish looked hopelessly beaten.

Then Montana drew on a reserve of energy and talent. A startling transformation began to take place. Montana hit Kris Haines on a 57-yard touchdown pass on Notre Dame's second play of the fourth quarter. It was USC 24, Notre Dame 12.

With almost seven minutes left and the ball on Notre Dame's two, Montana directed a 14-play, 98-yard drive, with Pete Buchanan scoring from the one. There was 3:01 left, and USC led, 24–19.

Notre Dame got the ball back on its 43 with 1:35 left, and Montana continued his magic. The Irish moved 57 yards in seven plays, with Pete Holohan catching a two-yard touchdown pass to put Notre Dame on top, 25–24.

There were 46 seconds left, Notre Dame fans were deliriously happy, convinced that their team had turned defeat into victory.

But USC wasn't finished. Taking over the ball on their 30 with 40 seconds left, the Trojans desperately tried to reach field-goal position. First, quarterback Paul McDonald completed a ten-yard sideline pass to tight end Vic Rakhshani. There was an incompleted pass that was perilously close to being a lost fumble when the ball was knocked out of McDonald's hand while passing.

With USC given new life, McDonald found Calvin Sweeney sprinting in the Notre Dame secondary. Sweeney made the catch for a 35-yard gain to the Irish 25. There were 12 seconds left.

Notre Dame quarterback Joe Montana. (Photo courtesy of Notre Dame Sports Information Department.)

Charles White ran five yards up the middle. USC called time-out. There were six seconds left, and onto the field came kicker Frank Jordan. Nothing was certain, because Jordan had missed a 20-yard field goal earlier in the quarter. But the snap and hold were perfect, and so was Jordan's 37-yard field goal with two seconds left, ending an unforgettable, fourth-quarter struggle.

USC running back Charles White. (Photo courtesy of USC Sports Information Department.)

USC placekicker Frank Jordan. (Photo courtesy of USC Sports Information Department.)

"It was one of the most remarkable comebacks probably in the history of the game," said Notre Dame Coach Dan Devine afterward.[1]

"It's the greatest football game I've ever seen, but maybe every USC–Notre Dame game is," remarked USC Coach John Robinson.[2]

USC, in the hunt for a national championship, improved to 10-1; Notre Dame fell to 8-3.

If greatness is measured by a player's performance under pressure, then Montana displayed those special qualities. In the first half, he completed 3 of 15 passes for 62 yards. In the second half, he hit 17 of 26 passes for 296 yards. Notre Dame had only five offensive possessions in the second half, and they ended with a field goal, fumble, touchdown, touchdown, touchdown. Haines caught nine passes for 179 yards.

On the other side of the ball, McDonald, a sophomore, completed 17 of 29 for 281 yards and two touchdowns. White carried 37 times for 205 yards.

Notre Dame Coach Dan Devine. (Photo courtesy of Notre Dame Sports Information Department.)

It was 60 minutes of thrills, but how ironic that with two seconds remaining, the game should be decided by the least athletic-looking player, a kicker named Jordan. This same kicker had beaten UCLA the previous year with two seconds left on a 38-yard field goal.

"I didn't really feel any pressure because I guess I was so involved watching the offense move the ball downfield," said Jordan in 1991. "I wasn't thinking that far ahead that suddenly I would be in the spotlight. I was just on the sideline stretching and trying to stay loose. It never occurred to me that within a matter of minutes, 90,000 people and 30 to 40 million people on TV were going to be watching me."

But Jordan knew USC was counting on him.

"Before the game, I was just standing on the sideline with the special-teams coach and we just watched the crowd filing into the stadium," he said. "And we were saying, 'Boy, this is what it's all about. This is college football at its best.'

"There's a certain kind of mystique, USC and Notre Dame. The atmosphere is incredible. During the game, the crowd noise is deafening.

There's never any silence. Either one side or the other is screaming or yelling."

Except when this game ended, both sides were too emotionally exhausted to scream.

Postscript: USC beat Michigan, 17–10, in the Rose Bowl to finish 12-1 and win a share of the national championship. The Associated Press voted Alabama No. 1, with United Press International giving the No. 1 vote to the Trojans. Notre Dame defeated Houston, 35–34, in the Cotton Bowl to finish 9-3. Notre Dame's victory over Houston was remarkably similar to the USC game, except that this time the Irish won, overcoming a 34–12 deficit in the final 7:37.

White won the Heisman Trophy the following season. In four years with the Trojans, White rushed for 100 or more yards 31 times. Jordan received tryouts with the Los Angeles Rams and Oakland Raiders but ended up going into the insurance business in the Bay Area.

Montana moved on to the National Football League, helping the San Francisco 49ers become the team of the 1980s with Super Bowl championships in the 1981, 1984, 1988 and 1989 seasons.

References

1. *Los Angeles Times,* 26 November 1978.
2. Ibid.

Hayes' Punch Mars Gator Bowl
Clemson 17, Ohio State 15 • December 29, 1978

Clemson middle guard Charlie Bauman intercepted only one pass during the season, but it came in the Gator Bowl, provoking Ohio State Coach Woody Hayes to slug him in the face on the sideline.

Bauman, a sophomore, sealed Clemson's 17–15 victory with his interception in the closing minute. He was tackled in front of the Ohio State bench, then attacked by Hayes, the Buckeyes' fiery, 65-year-old

Ohio State Coach Woody Hayes. (Photo courtesy of Ohio State Sports Information Department.)

coach. Afterward, Bauman was dazed and embarrassed by the incident as media surrounded him with questions. He was reluctant to even admit something had happened.

"If it happened, I'm not gonna say anything about it," he said. "I don't think he [Hayes] should be out there coaching. I know Woody has been known to do things like that."[1]

What Hayes did was hit Bauman in the face before being pulled off by an assistant coach. He drew two unsportsmanlike-conduct penalties for raging at officials and then instigating a brawl.

"Here we are in the huddle with 50 seconds to go in the ballgame," recalled Clemson quarterback Steve Fuller in 1991. "We have to run the clock out to win a big football game and the first conversations we had were, 'God, did you all see what happened? I think he hit him.' I had to say, 'Listen guys, that's fine and dandy, but we'll worry about it after we make a couple first downs.'"

Hayes refused comment after the incident, locking himself in an office. But Athletic Director Hugh Hindman knew that Hayes needed to be replaced.

The two had a bitter exchange in the locker room. According to Hindman, Hayes "asked if he had opportunity to resign and I told him he did. Shortly afterward, he said, 'I'm not going to resign. That would make it too easy for you. You had better go ahead and fire me.'"[2]

Hindman met with School President Harold Enarson much of the night before deciding to fire Hayes. "There is not a university or athletic conference in this country which would permit a coach to physically assault a college athlete," said Enarson.[3]

Hayes, who worshipped Gen. George S. Patton and kept a picture of baseball great Pete Rose on his office wall, joked years later about the incident, saying, "If I'd meant to hit him, I would have thrown a left."

As for Bauman, he did not want the spotlight and Clemson Coach Danny Ford advised him not to say anything about the incident, according to Fuller.

"He [Ford] grabbed Charlie and said, 'I know what happened, you know what happened. It's not important. Say it wasn't a very nice thing to do, but it's not going to help us by talking about it. Let it go and let other people form their opinions about it,'" Fuller said.

"I'm not saying they sheltered Charlie in the locker room, but they basically told him it's not important to talk about it right now."

Looking back at the incident 13 years later, Fuller said, "It's fun to laugh about it and joke about it right now.

"It was a neat thing for him [Bauman] because he will be forever remembered as the guy who ended Woody Hayes' career. But you look back and here's a guy who affected so many people's lives in 40-plus years of coaching.

"It was actually a very sad thing to see it happen. You didn't want to joke about it and pat him [Bauman] on the back and say, 'Gosh, you're going to be remembered forever for this.'"

Running back Archie Griffin, who played for Hayes from 1972–75 and won two Heisman Trophies, said in 1991, "A lot of people criticized the man, but the man did a lot more for the game of college football than any I could think of."

Postscript: One day later, Hayes was fired, ending a glorious but controversial 28 years as Buckeye coach.

The Hayes' altercation overshadowed Clemson's victory. Clemson, showing signs of becoming a national power, finished 11-1 and ranked sixth by the Associated Press. Three years later, the Tigers won their first national championship in a 12-0 season. "The sad thing is from that moment on and even through today, the only thing anybody remembers about the football game is what happened at the end," Fuller said. "Talk about private celebrations. No one nationally could tell you anything about the football game."

Hayes died in 1987 at 74. His 33-year college coaching record was 238-72-10, with two national championships, 13 Big Ten Conference titles and eight Rose Bowl appearances.

Bauman completed his athletic eligibility at Clemson, then never played again. He called the Clemson sports information department office after Hayes' death to say he did not want to talk to reporters.

Ford guided the Tigers to the national title in 1981, then resigned after the 1989 season after continued troubles involving NCAA investigations into the Clemson football program.

Ohio State finished 7-3-1 and was not ranked by AP.

References

1. The Associated Press, 30 December 1978.
2. Ibid.
3. Ibid.

Notre Dame, Montana
Dazzling in Fourth Quarter

Notre Dame 35, Houston 34 • January 1, 1979

Imagine a worst-case scenario for a football team and Notre Dame faced it against Houston in the Cotton Bowl.

The Fighting Irish trailed, 20–12, at halftime on a cold, windy morning in Dallas. Senior quarterback Joe Montana had thrown two interceptions in the first half and was shivering with the flu. Notre Dame Coach Dan Devine didn't know if Montana would play in the second half. Montana was fed hot chicken soup at halftime and given a warm shower in an effort to boost his below-normal body temperature and win clearance from the team doctor. Even when Montana returned, Notre Dame fell behind by 22 points with eight minutes remaining against the Southwest Conference champion.

"We knew for a fact people were clicking off their TVs all over the country," Notre Dame center Dave Huffman said in 1991. "You could hear the ratings drop every time Houston went up another point.

"It was so cold my dad left at halftime. He's a coward. He looked at my mom, 'I love you, I love the children, I have to get warm.' He spent the second half in the bathroom."

Notre Dame, however, came out of the cold to overcome a 34–12 deficit in the final 7:37 and edge Houston, 35–34, before a sparse crowd of 32,500.

"As far as comebacks were concerned, this one was unbelievable," Devine said about perhaps the greatest comeback in Notre Dame's fabled football history.

Despite Notre Dame's long odds at the end, Devine remained hopeful, grabbing players and coaches and telling them, "We're going to win." That's what head coaches are supposed to do, but that doesn't mean his players really believed him.

But in the last eight minutes of the final quarter, the strangest things started to happen. With 7:37 remaining in the game, Notre Dame's Tony Belden blocked a punt that was caught in midair by freshman Steve Cichy, who ran it back 33 yards for a touchdown. A two-point conversion made the score Houston 34, Notre Dame 20.

With 4:22 left, Montana ran two yards around left end for a touchdown, then threw a two-point conversion pass to Kris Haines to close the deficit to 34–28.

Montana got the ball back again and began driving Notre Dame to a potential winning touchdown. With 1:50 remaining, Houston linebacker David Hodge knocked the ball away from Montana and Houston's Tommy Ebner made the recovery on the Cougar 20. Now, there was no way Notre Dame could win, right?

"My mom is sitting there," said Huffman. "She's got three blankets around her. She's got a coat on. She's freezing, but she's not going to leave her baby on the field. And you could hear her. She's sitting 20 rows above me, and if there were 1,500 people in the stands, I would be surprised. You could hear her crying out, 'It's okay, baby, you'll come back.' We're getting beat up and you can carry on a conversation with her."

Houston players were celebrating and Notre Dame players were disillusioned. But Houston was unable to run out the clock. With 46 seconds remaining, Houston moved into punt formation, but the Irish were penalized for offsides, and Houston decided to go for the first down on fourth and one on its 29.

But Emmett King was stopped by Joe Gramke while trying to run over the left side and Notre Dame gained possession with 28 seconds remaining. Four plays later, as time expired and the gun was being shot off, Montana fired an eight-yard touchdown pass to Haines, tying the score at 34. All Notre Dame needed was the conversion kick from Joe Unis to win, but it wouldn't be easy.

The Irish picked up an illegal-procedure penalty, forcing Unis to attempt a 25-yard kick for the winning point. He made it. The game was over. Notre Dame had won.

"I felt complete exhilaration," Devine said in 1991.

It was Devine's complete trust in Montana that enabled the Irish to pull out the victory. With six seconds remaining and the ball on Houston's eight-yard line, Devine advised Montana on what to do.

"I gave Joe two plays," Devine said. "The first play I said, 'Run a '91,' which is a three-step drop, quick release, quick turnout by both wide receivers, drive down the corner and break out hoping on the poor turf you lose your defender.

"I said, 'Use the '91' and then come back with what you're most comfortable with. That might have been the smartest thing I did.

"Joe got rid of the ball because no one was there, leaving two seconds left. He kept looking at the bench for approval to come back with '91. I had a policy if I turned my back on a player, that told him he knew more about it than I did, that he should make the decision. I turned my back on Joe, and he came back with the same play. Joe always did what the coaches wanted him to do. That was a case maybe he was carrying it too far."

But the play worked, with Montana rolling right and getting the ball to Haines in the corner of the end zone. Notre Dame had accomplished the seemingly impossible.

"We had so many great comebacks at Notre Dame that it's so hard to say which is the greatest," Devine said, "but if I had to pick one, the combination of three touchdowns and two two-point extra points and one extra point in the final 7½ minutes..."

Postscript: Notre Dame (9-3) finished seventh in the nation and Houston (9-3) 10th in The Associated Press rankings. Devine retired from coaching after the 1980 season to spend more time with his wife, who was battling multiple sclerosis. In six seasons with the Irish, Devine had a record of 53-16-1. Devine became Missouri's athletic director in 1992.

Montana was a third-round draft choice of the San Francisco 49ers, for whom he earned the reputation as perhaps the best-ever National Football League quarterback, guiding the 49ers to Super Bowl victories in the 1981, 1984, 1988 and 1989 seasons. Notre Dame's offensive unit included future NFL players Dave and Tim Huffman (line), Pete Holohan (tight end) and Vagas Ferguson (running back). On the Irish defense was linebacker Bob Golic, a future star with the Cleveland Browns and the Los Angeles Raiders.

Alabama's Defense
Pins Penn State
Alabama 14, Penn State 7 • January 1, 1979

An old football saying is "defense makes champions."

In the Sugar Bowl battle between No. 1–ranked Penn State and

No. 2 Alabama in New Orleans' Superdome before 76,824 fans, that maxim was borne out.

Penn State's defense was excellent, but Alabama's was even better. The Crimson Tide posted a 14–7 victory in which its defense shut down Penn State's running attack and shut off the Nittany Lions' vaunted aerial attack triggered by All-American quarterback Chuck Fusina.

It was a forgettable day for Fusina, who without a running attack worth speaking about, hurled 30 passes, but completed only half for 163 yards with four interceptions. And he was unceremoniously sacked five times for minus 70 yards.

Yet, no one was hanging this loss squarely on Fusina's shoulders. It seemed as if he had little chance against the swarming, ubiquitous Crimson Tide defensive players who harried Fusina unmercifully throughout the game.

Alabama's 65-year-old head coach, Paul (Bear) Bryant, an offensive expert, had not worked on defense in years, but he cited his defense first as the key to the victory. "They took it to them," said Bryant afterward.[1]

Alabama's defensive dominance became crystal clear midway through the fourth quarter when the Crimson Tide put on a memorable goal-line stand. Trailing, 14–7, Penn State recovered an Alabama fumble at the Crimson Tide 19 and marched to the two-foot line after Fusina hit split end Scott Fitzkee on a five-yard pass.

With two downs remaining, Penn State seemed on the brink of scoring its second touchdown of the second half after failing to produce a point the entire first half.

On third down, fullback Matt Suhey got the call. He bulled into the Alabama middle and was stopped by linebacker Rich Wingo after traveling a mere 18 inches. He was six inches short of the goal line, prompting Fusina to call time-out and confer with Head Coach Joe Paterno.

On fourth down, Fusina handed the ball to tailback Mike Guman for another crack at Alabama's middle. This time linebacker Barry Krauss went underneath to stop Guman short of a touchdown.

"Alabama just beat us on the line of scrimmage," Paterno said afterward. "We should have been able to bang it in from there."[2]

"Our team beat a great football team," said Bryant. "Our entire squad contributed. I have never been associated with a group that did a greater job than our defense did today against Penn State."[3]

Senior halfback Tony Nathan, one of Alabama's offensive stars, expressed confidence that the Crimson Tide could hold Penn State during Alabama's pivotal goal-line stand.

"Our defense practices against us and we felt we had one of the top offenses," said Nathan in 1991. "So we felt if they could stop us, they could stop anyone."

And so went Penn State's bid for its first national championship. Paterno and Penn State fans had felt slighted when their undefeated teams failed to receive the No. 1 vote in 1969 and 1973.

But there could be no complaining this time.

"Alabama has as much a right to the national championship as anyone," Paterno said. "I think they beat an awfully good team today. I'm not disappointed for me. I'm disappointed for the players and particularly the seniors."[4]

Nathan led Alabama's offense by ripping off several substantial gains against the nation's No. 1–rated defense. He finished with 127 yards in 21 carries. Alabama quarterback Jeff Rutledge threw for only 91 yards, but he directed an 80-yard drive in 71 seconds that broke a scoreless tie in the last minute of the first half. Rutledge completed a 30-yard pass to split end Bruce Bolton for the touchdown that gave Alabama a 7–0 lead.

The drive was abetted by two consecutive time-outs, perhaps ill-advised, that Paterno called while Alabama had the ball in Crimson Tide territory. The first time-out was called on second and seven at Alabama's 23 with a minute remaining; the second was called with 49 seconds left and the Crimson Tide on the move. Nathan countered with runs of 30 and 7 yards to bring the ball to the Penn State 30.

"We were trying to stop the clock because we thought we could get a pass [completion] and then maybe a 50-yard field goal," Paterno said. "It just didn't work out."[5]

Penn State, however, regained the momentum in the third quarter after safety Pete Harris intercepted a Rutledge pass at the Alabama 48. Fusina then marched his team to the tying touchdown. He hit Fitzkee at the back edge of the end zone for a 17-yard touchdown to lift Penn State into a 7–7 tie.

The momentum reshifted later in the quarter when Alabama halfback Lou Ikner ran a punt back 62 yards, taking the ball to the Penn State 11-yard line. Three plays later, halfback Major Ogilvie scored from eight yards out to give Alabama the lead for good at 14–7.

Alabama Coach Paul (Bear) Bryant. (Photo courtesy of Alabama Sports Information Department.)

Penn State's final chance was rubbed out by penalty with six minutes remaining in the game. A 12-yard Alabama punt appeared to have left the Nittany Lions in great field position at the Alabama 30. But the punt was wiped out because Penn State had 12 men on the field. And a 13th Penn State player barely got off the field in time.

It was that kind of a day for Penn State.

Postscript: Alabama (11-1) was named the United Press International's national champion, although USC earned the No. 1 vote from the Associated Press. USC had defeated Alabama, 24–14, during the regular season, but the Trojans (12-1) had lost to new Pac-10 member Arizona State early in the season. Penn State (11-1) dropped to fourth in the AP voting.

Fusina was second in the Heisman Trophy voting with 750 points, finishing behind Oklahoma running back Billy Sims, who had 827 points. Penn State defensive tackle Bruce Clark received the Lombardi Award, which is given to the nation's best lineman.

Nathan became a standout running back for the Miami Dolphins and Suhey distinguished himself at fullback for the Chicago Bears.

References

1. *Los Angeles Times,* 2 January 1979.
2. Ibid.
3. Gene Brown, *The New York Scrapbook Encyclopedia of Sports History — The Complete Book of Football* (Indianapolis/New York: Bobbs-Merrill Company, Inc., 1980).
4. Ibid.
5. *Los Angeles Times,* 2 January 1979.

BYU Celebrates
Holiday Bowl Comeback
Brigham Young 46, Southern Methodist 45
December 19, 1980

With 4:07 remaining, Brigham Young's chances of overcoming a 45–25 deficit against Southern Methodist in the Holiday Bowl looked undeniably bleak.

But those among the crowd of 50,214 who loyally stuck around until the end witnessed a remarkable turnaround. In a matter of 2:33, BYU scored 21 points, including a 41-yard touchdown pass from Jim McMahon to Clay Brown on the game's final play that lifted the Cougars to a 46–45 victory at Jack Murphy Stadium in San Diego.

"If that game had been on national TV, people would probably be still writing it up today," BYU Coach LaVelle Edwards said 11 years later.

The comeback becomes more improbable considering SMU possessed the ideal personnel to run out the clock. The Mustangs were led by running backs Craig James and Eric Dickerson, who combined to rush for 335 yards and five touchdowns.

SMU's problem was that it couldn't hang onto the ball. After James scored on a 42-yard run with 4:07 left to give SMU its 20-point lead, BYU scored on a touchdown pass; recovered an onside kick and scored on a one-yard run by Scott Phillips; and blocked a punt and scored on McMahon's desperation pass to the 6-foot-3, 230-pound Brown.

"That was the greatest game I've ever been involved in," said Brown in 1991.

Trailing by six points, BYU took over the ball with 18 seconds left on SMU's 41-yard line after a blocked punt by Bill Schoepflin. After two long passes fell incomplete, BYU used its "save-the-game pass."

"It was like any Hail Mary pass. You just tell the receivers to run deep and everyone else stays in and blocks so you can get maximum protection," Edwards said.

Two BYU receivers raced downfield from their end positions and converged toward the middle. Brown, the tight end, simply ran straight up the middle.

"It was just a free-for-all," Brown said. "McMahon threw that thing so high, it was incredible. I caught it in full stride. I just had to turn and jump up. There were four defenders right there. One guy was trying to catch the ball, which he should never have done. It went right through his hands. Timing was crucial.

"The catch itself was the easy part. I wasn't really fighting for the ball coming down, but when I was down on the ground, a couple guys latched on and it was a major, major struggle while the refs were unpiling.

"I don't know if I worked as hard as trying to hold the ball. It seemed like it took ten minutes to unpile us. Man, there was a lot of yanking on that ball."

The officials finally signaled that Brown had made the catch in the end zone for the touchdown, leaving it to kicker Kurt Gunther to deliver the winning conversion point. Brigham Young fans became delirious. Even the mild-mannered Edwards couldn't believe the Cougars'

Brigham Young quarterback Jim McMahon. (Photo courtesy of Brigham Young Sports Information Department.)

160   Brigham Young 46, Southern Methodist 45 (1980)

remarkable comback. Only a half-hour earlier, Edwards was feeling miserable.

"This was the fifth bowl game we had been to and we had never won one," he said. "Leading up to it, everybody is saying, 'This is it, I got a feeling you're going to win.' I don't think I had ever gone into a game where I personally felt more pressure. I remember thinking sometime in the middle of the third quarter, 'Geez, I hope I never go to another bowl game.'"

SMU's offensive firepower on the ground was devastating. James rushed for 225 yards in 23 carries and scored three touchdowns. Dickerson gained 110 carries in 23 carries and scored two touchdowns.

Countering SMU's rushing game was McMahon, a junior who emerged as the nation's most prolific quarterback. McMahon, showing his great leadership and competitive fire, completed 32 of 49 passes for 446 yards and three touchdowns. Brown caught five passes for 155 yards and three touchdowns.

During one crucial BYU drive in the fourth quarter, Edwards decided to punt rather than go for a first down on a fourth-and-two situation. The always-vocal McMahon stormed off the field, upset at the decision. It caused Edwards to take a time-out and re-evaluate. He changed his mind, electing not to punt. BYU made the first down and later a touchdown.

"I've often thought about it," Edwards said. "I'm not totally sure I would have called a time-out and made the decision to go for it if McMahon had not stormed off."

Postscript: Brigham Young finished 12-1 and received its first national recognition as a football program on the rise, ranking 12th by the Associated Press. In 1984, the Cougars would go 13-0 and win the national championship. McMahon led the nation in passing with 4,571 yards and 47 touchdowns in 1980. In his four-year college career, McMahon set school records by passing for 9,536 yards and 84 touchdowns. He joined the Chicago Bears in 1982 and led them to a 46–10 Super Bowl victory over the New England Patriots in 1985.

SMU, which made its first bowl appearance in 12 years, finished 8-4 and was ranked 20th by AP. James went on to play for the Patriots. Dickerson emerged as one of the National Football League's great running backs. He was the second player selected in the 1983 draft. In his first season for the Los Angeles Rams, he rushed for 1,808 yards, a rookie record. The next year, he broke O. J. Simpson's single-season record with 2,105 yards. Another big-time player for SMU was nose guard Michael Carter, who became a key defensive player for the San Francisco 49ers during their glory years of the 1980s.

Alabama's "Bear" Makes His Mark

Alabama 28, Auburn 17 • *November 28, 1981*

Bear Bryant couldn't have been happier.

Not only did he set a major-college record for career coaching victories with Alabama's 28–17 win over Auburn before 78,170 fans at Birmingham, Alabama, but he achieved it in a manner that made him extremely proud of his team.

Alabama fashioned two well-executed touchdown drives in the fourth quarter to overcome both a three-point deficit and its state rival. For Bryant, victory No. 315 in his 37th year as coach may have been difficult to achieve, but that just made the historic victory a little bit sweeter.

"I like coming from behind," said Bryant afterward. "Give me my druthers and we'll come from behind like that. It proved to our players that they have class and character, and it showed them what can be done in the future."[1]

Bryant eclipsed Amos Alonzo Stagg as the winningest coach with Alabama's ninth consecutive win over the Tigers. It marked the end of the regular season for the Crimson Tide (9-1-1) and brought to a halt the long-held anticipation of the record win.

How much was Alabama thinking about the record during the game? "Every time we lined up in the fourth quarter," said Alabama defensive back Benny Perrin afterward, "we would say in the huddle, 'We can't give up. This is for "315" and the record.'"[2]

Alabama's All-American defensive back Tommy Wilcox took a slightly different view. He said that winning—not breaking the record—was the pre-eminent theme during the game. And it was a theme created by none other than the 68-year-old Bryant.

"Coach Bryant played [the record] down," said Wilcox in 1991. "All week he had us focusing on Auburn and not '315' and thought that the record would take care of itself sooner or later. Although we were focused on Alabama, the record was still in the back of our minds. I'm sure it was."

The record became more tangible after Alabama put together a seven-play, 75-yard touchdown drive and a three-play, 49-yard drive in the final quarter. Bryant's marvelous skills as a coach were evident in all four of Alabama's scoring drives, which featured:

- A 63-yard quarterback sweep by Alan Gray that set up Alabama's first touchdown and gave the Crimson Tide a 6-0 first-quarter lead.
- A 26-yard shovel pass on second and fifteen from quarterback Ken Coley to Jesse Bendross that gave Alabama its second touchdown and a 14-7 third-quarter lead.
- A 38-yard touchdown pass from quarterback Walter Lewis to Bendross in the fourth quarter that put Alabama ahead, 21-17. It was a first-down, play-action pass, and Auburn was fooled by the fake.
- Runs of 32 and 15 yards by Linnie Patrick in Alabama's final touchdown drive, lifting Alabama into a 28-17 lead.

One of the pivotal plays of the game came in the first quarter when Wilcox blunted an Auburn threat with an interception. Alabama went on to score first, taking a 7-0 first-quarter lead on Gray's one-yard run.

"In a game where you're facing an in-state rival, momentum can swing so fast," Wilcox said. "We went from seven points down to seven points ahead."

Auburn, however, recovered from the 7-0 deficit to tie the score, 7-7, in the second quarter on George Peoples' 63-yard run. Alabama retook the lead in the third quarter, 14-7, but Auburn moved back into a tie after recovering a fumble at Alabama's two-yard line.

All told, Alabama lost three fumbles in the third quarter and Auburn capitalized on the last one to grab a 17-14 lead early in the fourth quarter.

That's when Alabama's offense started to grind out the yards and take command.

"I don't think it was the best football game we played in my four years there," Wilcox said, "but under the circumstances, we did what we had to do."

Bryant addressed reporters after the game without his trademark houndstooth hat, which had been stolen the moment the game had ended. Bryant said it was difficult to reflect on the significance of his historic win.

"It hasn't set in yet," Bryant said. "I feel like I ought to go back and check the scoreboard to make sure we won."[3]

Alabama's players didn't need a second look. They were too busy rejoicing and sharing in their coach's triumph. For this was a coach whom the players not only liked but greatly respected.

"From a team standpoint, everyone respected him," Wilcox said. "He was just a great person to play for. I wish a lot of other young people had the chance to play for Bear Bryant.

"He taught you about sacrificing and work habits, things you could use later in your life. I think people sometimes were afraid of him, but they always respected him. Everyone who played for Bear Bryant played their hearts out for him. One of his intangibles was that he got everyone to play over his head."

Postscript: Alabama, ranked seventh by the Associated Press, finished the season with a 9-2-1 record after a 14-12 loss to Texas in the Cotton Bowl. Alabama was 8-4 the following season in Bryant's final year of coaching, the first time in 11 seasons the Crimson Tide failed to finish in the top 20.

Alabama's final victory of the 1982 season came in the Liberty Bowl when the Crimson Tide defeated Illinois, 21-15. Bryant retired from coaching after the game. He died less than one month later at 69.

Said Bryant after the win over Illinois: "I am thankful to have won my final game. Whether the team likes it or not, they will always be remembered for winning my last game. I am proud they wanted to win this one for me."[4]

Bryant's career record stood at 323-85-17. He coached at Maryland (1945), Kentucky (1946–53), Texas A&M (1954–57) and Alabama (1958–82).

References

1. *Los Angeles Times,* 24 November 1981.
2. Ibid.
3. Ibid.
4. *Alabama 1990 Football Press Guide.*

Five Laterals Later, Cal Prevails
Cal 25, Stanford 20 • November 20, 1982

It was one of the most laughable, outlandish and whimsical endings imaginable, this 85th meeting between Stanford and Cal at Memorial Stadium in Berkeley.

With four seconds left, Stanford took a 20–19 lead on Mark Harmon's 35-yard field goal. Then came the real entertainment.

Kicking off from his 25 after Stanford incurred a 15-yard unsportsmanlike-conduct penalty, Harmon booted a squib kick that was grabbed by Cal's Kevin Moen at his 43. He started running, was about to be tackled and then lateraled to Richard Rodgers, who lateraled to Dwight Garner at the Cal 44. Garner was about to be pulled down by three tacklers when he lateraled to Rodgers at the Cal 48. Rodgers then lateraled to Mariet Ford at the Stanford 48.

All this time, Stanford fans and its band began to inch onto the field, preparing to celebrate victory. But the game was still going on. Ford had the ball and was suddenly trapped at the Stanford 25. Out of desperation, he flipped the ball over his shoulder and Moen caught it and headed toward the end zone. Now, fans and band members were on the field. Moen got past a tuba player, then ran over a trombone player in the end zone to score a bizarre touchdown, giving Cal an unforgettable 25–20 victory in both teams' season finales.

Officials huddled for five minutes after the 57-yard, five-lateral kickoff return, then ruled it good. Afterward, the Stanford band was embarrassed and players were in shock.

"What a farce," said Stanford quarterback John Elway afterward. "This was an insult to college football. There's no way it should have happened. They [the officials] ruined my last college football game. It's unbelievable."[1]

A distraught Stanford Coach Paul Wiggin said afterward, "In our hearts and our minds, we won the game."[2]

But on the scoreboard, the Bears won, and nothing they did was judged illegal. The officials never ruled that any of Cal's players who had the ball was down. As for fans and band members on the field, they were from Stanford, and the Cardinal would have been penalized on the play.

"Why did it work? Because we never practiced it," Moen said nine years later. "We just did it. It just so happened the pieces fit together. You've seen people attempt to do this stuff all the time, try to lateral the ball. Even doing it once or twice is hard. To do it five times is almost impossible."

Moen was never told to start lateraling after he received the kick-off, although several other Cal players were instructed to do anything they could to keep the ball alive.

The team did have one advantage — the Bears were used to laterals.

"We played this game on Sundays — garbazz," Moen said. "It was for getting loose and running out the soreness. There would be 20 guys on each side and we would keep lateraling."

Some spontaneous thinking by all the players involved resulted in the successful play.

"When I got the ball, I just basically said, 'Hey, I've got nowhere to go. I might as well find somebody,'" Moen said. "I just happened to see Richard Rodgers along the sideline and chucked it to him. He had nowhere to go and then it kind of caught on. Everybody got the essence of what needed to be done."

As for running over a Stanford trombone player and juking a tuba player, Moen said, "It didn't hurt my feelings knocking over the trombone player. He just happened to be in the wrong place at the wrong time."

Even when Moen finally reached the end zone, he did not realize Cal had won. Pandemonium had broken out on the field.

"As soon as it happened, it was so confusing," he said. "I really didn't have a grip on what happened. I knew there was a bunch of laterals. Right when I scored, I got completely mobbed in the end zone. I just sat down at the goal posts to catch my breath. All of a sudden, I heard the school cannon go off and at that point I knew it was good.

"The further in time it gets, the more unique that play becomes. I don't think it has been rivaled with the situation, the circumstances of the band coming out — all those ingredients. I don't think it's something you could predict or plan to do. It was something that just happened."

Almost forgotten was Stanford's comeback after trailing, 10–0, at the end of the first half.

Elway passed for 260 of his 330 yards in the second half. Altogether, he completed 25 of 39, including two third-quarter touchdowns that put Stanford ahead, 14–10. Cal quarterback Gale Gilbert passed

Cal's Kevin Moen. (Photo courtesy of California Sports Information Department.)

for 289 yards, including a 32-yard touchdown pass to Wes Howell that gave the Bears a 19–14 lead in the fourth quarter.

But everything that happened before the final kickoff became secondary.

A few years later, Moen was playing touch football and got his team to try another lateral play. "It didn't work," he said. "How many times does something like that work?"

Postscript: Stanford finished 5-6 and lost out on a bid to the Hall of Fame Bowl because of the defeat. Cal finished 7-4. Elway ended the season passing for 3,242 yards and 24 touchdowns. He wound up his college career by passing for 9,349 yards and 77 touchdowns. He finished second to Georgia's Herschel Walker in the Heisman Trophy balloting. Elway was the first player taken in the 1983 National Football League draft by the Baltimore Colts, then was traded to the Denver Broncos, where he emerged as one of the league's greatest quarterbacks. Moen tried to make the NFL as a free agent but failed and went into the real estate business in Southern California.

Stanford Coach Paul Wiggin was fired after a 1-10 season in 1983.

References

1. *Los Angeles Times*, 21 November 1982.
2. Ibid.

Miami Beats "Unbeatable" Nebraska

Miami 31, Nebraska 30 • January 2, 1984

As psyche jobs go, Miami Coach Howard Schnellenberger deserved credit for a performance that Sigmund Freud would have admired.

His opponent, No. 1–ranked Nebraska, was 12-0, had a 22-game winning streak and was averaging 52 points per game entering the Orange Bowl game in Miami. The Cornhuskers were being compared to the best teams of the 1970s and 1980s and were an 11-point favorite. But on this night, the entire city of Miami believed Schnellenberger's third-ranked Hurricanes would win. Even Nebraska Coach Tom Osborne felt uneasy.

"Howard Schnellenberger did a tremendous job mobilizing the community down there," said Osborne in 1991. "He made people who had never seen a Miami football game think of themselves as alums. It was a difficult environment to play in."

What happened was a game for the ages. Miami stormed to a 17–0 lead in the first quarter, was up, 17–14, at halftime, opened a 31-17 advantage going into the fourth quarter, then barely held on for a 31–30 victory before 72,549 fans.

Credit Schnellenberger for convincing his players they could beat

Miami Coach Howard Schnellenberger. (Photo courtesy of Miami Sports Information Department.)

a Nebraska team that had looked unbeatable during the season. The Cornhuskers weren't just beating opponents — they were thrashing them. They clobbered Minnesota, 84–13, triumphed over Colorado, 69–19, and crushed Iowa State, 72–19.

Yet Schnellenberger told a *Sports Illustrated* reporter before the game that his team was "about to face the Russian army, and they don't care. They think they're going to win. And I'm the silly bastard who has everybody around here thinking they will. That's okay. I think so too."

Nebraska pulled to within 31–30 with 48 seconds left on tailback Jeff Smith's 24-yard touchdown run. Rather than go for a tie, Osborne decided to go for the victory with a two-point conversion play. A tie undoubtedly would have won the national title for the Cornhuskers, but Osborne refused to play it safe.

"I thought if you were going to win a national championship, you had to win," he said.

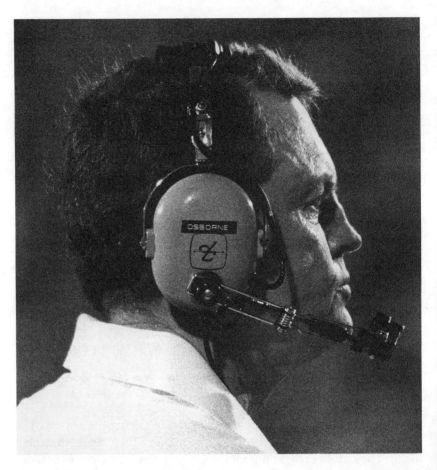

Nebraska Coach Tom Osborne. (Photo courtesy of Nebraska Sports Information Department.)

So Osborne had quarterback Turner Gill try to deliver a victory by passing. Gill rolled right and tried to hit Smith. The pass was a little behind Smith, and Miami roverback Kenny Calhoun got three fingers on the ball, deflecting it to the ground. The stadium erupted, with fans charging onto the field to celebrate despite time still left on the clock.

Seven years later, Osborne said he still believes he made the right decision.

"I don't think I would do it differently," he said. "I don't think our players would have felt good about a tie. I think they would have always felt they could have won the game. As it was, it was just a matter of a guy getting a finger on the football. The receiver was there. I think the play was well-conceived."

Looking back in 1991, Schnellenberger said he is proud about what his team accomplished. He had come to Miami in 1979 after serving as an assistant coach with the Miami Dolphins. The Hurricanes' program wasn't regarded as national caliber, but by the end of the 1983 season, Schnellenberger had put together one of the nation's great success stories.

"South Florida had fallen in love with the football team," he said. "There was just a groundswell of support. You have to remember that the city of Miami had gone through some troubling times of civil disobedience. The team became a new positive force and the people came together behind it. It was a very unfair situation for Nebraska.

"It was the most electric environment I have ever been in. People were sending out vibes that were felt in the middle of the field and across the field."

No Miami player felt the positive vibes more than quarterback Bernie Kosar, who didn't have the powerful arm or quickness of a John Elway but always seemed to get the ball on target. Kosar picked apart the Nebraska defense, completing 19 of 35 passes for 300 yards. He threw for two touchdowns during a 17-0 Miami first quarter, both to tight end Glenn Dennison (2 and 22 yards).

Nebraska, despite its horrible start, was back in the game by halftime. The Cornhuskers had a backfield that Osborne believed was one of the best ever. With Gill at quarterback, Heisman Trophy winner Mike Rozier at tailback and Irving Fryar at wingback, Nebraska was capable of making big plays, but it was a trick play that gave the Cornhuskers renewed confidence.

Gill fumbled deliberately, with 270-pound guard Dean Steinkuhler picking up the ball and running 19 yards for a touchdown to make the score 17-7 in the second quarter. Schnellenberger criticized the play, saying, "It was devious and unsportsmanlike," but Nebraska needed it badly.

By early in the third quarter, Nebraska had tied the score at 17. But Miami (11-1) went back on the offensive behind the passing of Kosar and the running of freshman Alonzo Highsmith. Highsmith (one yard) and Albert Bentley (seven yards) each ran for touchdowns in the third quarter, putting Miami on top, 31-17.

The Cornhuskers closed to 31-24 on a one-yard run by Smith and when Miami missed a field-goal attempt, Nebraska got the ball back with 1:47 left. Gill quickly had the Cornhuskers on the move.

On fourth and eight from the Miami 24, Smith broke loose for a touchdown. Then came the dramatic two-point attempt.

"We made the call that put us in the best possible defense to make the play," Schnellenberger said. "Whether we were lucky or not, only God in his infinite wisdom knows."

Rozier gained 147 yards in 25 carries before leaving the game because of a twisted left ankle in the third quarter.

Postscript: Miami earned its first national championship after second-ranked Texas and fourth-ranked Illinois were beaten in bowl games. Miami's only loss came against Florida in its opening game. Schnellenberger resigned in May to take over a United States Football League franchise in Miami, but the team never became a reality. Schnellenberger's five-year record with the Hurricanes was 41-16.

In December 1984, he took over as head coach at Louisville. Miami became the team of the 1980s, also winning national titles in the 1987 and 1989 seasons under Jimmy Johnson and Dennis Erickson, respectively.

Kosar was taken by the Cleveland Browns in the 1985 supplemental draft and became one of the National Football League's best passers. Rozier won the Heisman Trophy for the 1983 season and was a first-round draft choice of the New England Patriots. Steinkuhler won the Outland Trophy as the nation's outstanding lineman.

Maryland's Miraculous Comeback
Maryland 42, Miami 40 • November 10, 1984

As far as great comebacks go, it ranked as the greatest of them all.

Maryland spotted Miami a 31–0 lead at halftime and charged back to win, 42–40, before 31,548 fans at Miami's Orange Bowl behind quarterback Frank Reich. According to NCAA records, Maryland's victory ranked as the No. 1 comeback in the history of major college football, surpassing Oregon State's rally from a 28–0 deficit to a 31–28 victory over Fresno State on September 12, 1981.

"We did the impossible because no one in the world would think we could come back from that many points behind against Miami," said Reich afterward.[1]

Reich masterminded the comeback after he replaced starter Stan Gelbaugh in the second half. The 6-foot-4 Reich completed 12 of 15 passes for 260 yards and three touchdowns and ran for a touchdown.

"We were embarrassed in the first half," Reich said. "No one likes to be embarrassed. We had to save our pride so we pulled together."[2]

Maryland could credit its offense — with its six-touchdown, second-half output — with the victory. But the Terrapins would have to credit their defense with the save.

With 50 seconds remaining in the game, Miami quarterback Bernie Kosar hit Ken Brown on a five-yard touchdown pass that allowed the defending national champion Hurricanes to close within two points at 42–40. Miami then went for the two-point conversion to try to tie the score. Kosar threw a pass to halfback Melvin Bratton, who made the reception but was immediately tackled short of the goal line by defensive back Keeta Covington.

"We were in zone defense," Covington said. "They had called the same play, and it had worked earlier but we were in a different coverage then. It was my zone and I saw the play clearly."[3]

Maryland's victory wiped out any hopes the sixth-ranked Hurricanes (8-3) had of winning a national title along with Miami's five-game winning streak. Maryland improved to 6-3 with its sixth victory in the past seven games. But the Terrapins' start was anything but auspicious.

Kosar riddled Maryland's defense for 240 passing yards and three touchdowns in lifting Miami into its 31-point lead at intermission. Miami had 19 first downs to Maryland's three and outgained the Terrapins, 328–57. But Kosar would prove human in the second half when Reich would turn superhuman.

Reich, a fifth-year senior, had lost his starting job six weeks earlier when he suffered a separated right shoulder and backup Gelbaugh performed magnificently in his place. But Reich regained his job with his whirlwind second-half performance that got off to an electrifying start when he threw a 39-yard touchdown pass to Greg Hill on his third play of the day.

That score pulled Maryland within 31–7. Reich then capped a 60-yard march with a 1-yard touchdown run to leave Maryland behind at 31–14, and by the time the third quarter ended, the Terrapins would trail by a less-than-insurmountable 34–21. Maryland would take the lead for good when Reich connected with Hill on a 68-yard touchdown bomb, putting the Terrapins into a 35–34 lead. Miami's Darrell Fullington tipped the pass, but Hill grabbed the deflection and dashed the final 30 yards to the end zone.

"When I let it go," Reich said, "I thought it might be too far. A while before, Greg said he could beat his man on a sprint-and-go. He told me, I told the coach who calls the plays and we came back with it. The wind held it up a little bit and Greg kept his concentration."[4]

After Miami fumbled the ensuing kickoff, Lewis Askew recovered at the five for Maryland. Two plays later, fullback Rick Badanjek scored from four yards out to put Maryland in command with a 42–34 lead.

"This is the most disappointing loss I have ever been associated with," a distraught Miami Coach Jimmy Johnson said afterward. "We just allowed them to get back in the game. I could sense in the third quarter they had the momentum, but we could never do anything about it."[5]

Meanwhile, Maryland Coach Bobby Ross was equally dismayed by his team's first-half performance. "The first half was a disaster," Ross said. "We just played better in the second half. I told them at halftime if we didn't do better in the second half, we would just get on the bus and we would have a practice tonight."[6]

That night, instead of practicing, Reich was wandering around the parking lot outside the Orange Bowl trying to meet up with a television crew eager to get his thoughts on his just-completed heroics.

During his search for the interviewer, Reich happened to bump into another key principal in the game: Miami Coach Johnson.

"You did a great job," Johnson told Reich. "That's something you'll remember the rest of your life."[7]

Postscript: Things did not get any better for Miami the following week. Boston College quarterback Doug Flutie threw a 65-yard touchdown pass to Gerard Phelan as time expired to hand Miami another heartbreaking loss, this time 47–45. The string of Miami losses then stretched to three when UCLA outscored the Hurricanes, 39–37, in the Fiesta Bowl. Miami (8-5) finished 18th in the Associated Press poll.

Maryland, meanwhile, ended up ranked 12th and 9-3 after a 27–26 Sun Bowl victory over Tennessee.

Maryland's record for biggest comeback was broken in 1986 by Morehead State, which rallied from a 32-point deficit to defeat Wichita State, 36–35. In 1991, Nevada-Reno broke the record again by rallying from a 35-point deficit to stun Weber State, 55–49.

References

1. *Los Angeles Times*, 11 November 1984.
2. Ibid.
3. *The Washington Post*, 11 November 1984.
4. Ibid.
5. *Los Angeles Times*, 11 November 1984.
6. Ibid.
7. *The Washington Post*, 11 November 1984.

Flutie's Fabulous Finish

Boston College 47, Miami 45 • November 23, 1984

On a rainy, windy Miami night, the day after Thanksgiving, a new term was coined. For the 30,235 fans at the Orange Bowl watching Miami play Boston College, "Hail Flutie" replaced "Hail Mary" in the American sports lexicon to describe a seemingly hopeless, last-second, last-ditch bomb.

There was Doug Flutie, a 5-foot-9¾ quarterback from Boston College, taking the final snap of an already memorable game. There were six seconds remaining, his team trailed by four points and the ball was on the Miami 48.

Everyone on the field and in the crowd knew that the tiny quarterback would try to throw deep. As Flutie dropped back to pass, three wide receivers stationed to the right raced downfield. The one in the middle was Flutie's favorite target, senior Gerard Phelan.

Phelan was a full step ahead of Miami defensive back Darrell Fullington at the ten, but Flutie was chased out of the pocket. He scrambled to his right and reached the 37-yard line, where he planted his left foot and let the ball fly.

Boston College quarterback Doug Flutie. (Photo courtesy of Jet Commercial Photographers Inc.)

176   Boston College 47, Miami 45 (1984)

Half the Hurricane defense was near the goal line, but the ball floated over the defenders' heads and was caught by Phelan as he fell on his back in the end zone. Boston College won, 47–45.

"After I threw the ball, I didn't see anything much until the referee raised his arms," Flutie said. "Then, I admit, I couldn't believe it, except when everybody started yelling and pulling me up."[1]

Miami, the defending national champion, entered the game with an 8-3 record. Boston College was 7-2 and possessed one of the nation's best offenses. The game was a passing circus.

Flutie completed 34 of 46 passes for 472 yards and three touchdowns. Miami sophomore Bernie Kosar completed 25 of 38 for 447 yards and two touchdowns. Phelan enjoyed the game of his life, catching 11 passes for 226 yards. Miami's Eddie Brown had 10 receptions for 220 yards. Miami running back Melvin Bratton rushed for 134 yards and scored four touchdowns.

"It was total offense," Phelan said in 1991. "Every time the defense would make a play, the offense would make a better play."

The game's ending was mind-boggling. Miami had taken the lead for what seemed to be the last time with 28 seconds left on Bratton's one-yard touchdown run. Who would have guessed that Flutie and Boston College still had a miracle up their sleeves? Who would have believed Flutie could throw a pass more than 64 yards on the fly.

"Most players I've seen when they get into that kind of position give up," Phelan said. "I don't think anybody on our team really thought that way from the beginning of the play to the end."

The last play was called "Flood Tip." The three Boston College receivers were supposed to arrive together at the same time, flood the zone and then tip the ball up in the air for one to retrieve. The play had worked against Temple earlier in the year.

"I guess the defenders didn't think Doug could throw the ball that far, and I knew he could," Phelan said. "As he threw it, the ball was coming down and as everybody jumped up in front of me, the ball disappeared for a moment and there was a lot of contact. All of a sudden, the ball reappeared, probably in the last three yards.

"It was one of those things where you react as quick as you can. Just like a fork falls off a table, you react to catch it. I happened to get it."

So ended a game that produced enough excitement for an entire week of games.

"It was the epitome of college football," Phelan said. "It also epitomized the underdog. I think Americans love to root for the underdog, and certainly Boston College and Doug Flutie were underdogs.

"Here was a scrambling, get-it-done-any-way-you-can kind of guy who had good grades and didn't get into trouble. Everybody was rooting for that guy to win."

Phelan also remembers the weather suddenly changing during the final play.

"It was rainy and the turf was soft, but during that particular play, the rain stopped," he said.

The ramifications of Boston College's victory were felt immediately.

"At one time, Boston College was kind of a Lilliputian school tucked up in New England not identifiable from Boston University," Phelan said. "Suddenly, it became a national focus and hero for a lot of people around the country. They could identify what college football stood for and what a student-athlete really is."

Postscript: Boston College beat Houston, 45–28, in the Cotton Bowl under Coach Jack Bicknell to finish 10-2 and ranked fifth by the Associated Press. Flutie won the Heisman Trophy with 2,240 votes. He became the first college quarterback to pass for more than 10,000 yards in his career. Flutie was selected in the 11th round of the National Football League draft by the Los Angeles Rams but signed to play for the New Jersey Generals of the United States Football League. Phelan was selected in the fourth round by the New England Patriots but never played a down after suffering a severe knee injury during training camp.

Bicknell was fired in 1990 after four consecutive losing seasons. Miami lost to UCLA, 39–37, in the Fiesta Bowl to finish 8-5 and 18th ranked by AP. Kosar placed fourth in the Heisman Trophy balloting and was selected by the Cleveland Browns in the 1985 supplemental draft after his sophomore season.

Reference

1. The Associated Press, 24 November 1984.

Iowa Gets Big
Kick Out of Victory

Iowa 12, Michigan 10 • October 19, 1985

For one bright, shining afternoon, legions of financially depressed farmers across Iowa were united in forgetting their troubles to focus on the battle between No. 1–ranked Iowa and No. 2–ranked Michigan in Iowa City.

A crowd of 66,350, setting a record for the largest attendance at a sporting event in Iowa, saw a game that lifted the morale of an entire state.

It came down to a 29-yard field goal. There were two seconds left, with Michigan leading, 10–9. Iowa kicker Rob Houghtlin could deliver victory or defeat. He had a sore leg that kept him out of practice for three weeks and he was a mere walk-on. But this was his moment of destiny.

Houghtlin made the field goal as time expired, giving Iowa a 12–10 Big Ten victory and setting off a celebration that would have dwarfed the wildest parties in New York.

"The place went bananas," said Iowa quarterback Chuck Long in 1991. "The stadium cleared, the goal posts came down. It was like a Hollywood ending."

It was Iowa's sixth straight victory, and nothing felt better for the Hawkeyes and their fans than to beat Michigan's irascible Bo Schembechler.

For Iowa Coach Hayden Fry, no win was sweeter. Fry had been fired by SMU before spending six years in exile at North Texas State. Now, this victory signified that Iowa was a national power and the team to beat in the Big Ten.

"I told Coach Schembechler before the game and repeated it after, 'It's too bad that one team had to lose this game,'" said Fry afterward. "I told him he had a great team, and he said, 'But you have the greatest.' That was quite a compliment coming from Coach Schembechler. He even gave me a pack of chewing gum."[1]

Iowa dominated the game, but the Hawkeyes had trouble scoring. They could not reach the end zone and ended up relying on four field

Iowa quarterback Chuck Long. (Photo courtesy of Iowa Sports Information Department.)

180   Iowa 12, Michigan 10 (1985)

goals by Houghtlin. They outgained Michigan, 422–182, and ran off 84 plays to the Wolverines' 41.

Still, it came down to one final drive orchestrated by Long, Iowa's senior quarterback who had turned down the National Football League to stay a fifth year and ended up purchasing a $1 million insurance policy in case of injury.

But Long was in control when Iowa took over the ball on its 22 with 5:27 left and Michigan ahead, 10–9.

"I knew we had a good passing game going, and it was just a matter of us not beating ourselves on that last drive," he said. "I knew we could get the ball downfield. We had a lot of confidence in the huddle. We had a lot of seniors and it was basically 'Do or Die, guys.' We got into the huddle and said, 'This is it. This is our season. We have to score.'"

Long combined short passes with the running of tailback Ronnie Harmon. The Hawkeyes were in no great hurry, preferring to use the clock to make sure Michigan didn't have another chance to handle the ball.

Finally, Harmon ran over right tackle for a gain of four yards to the Michigan 12, and Long called a time-out with two seconds left. It was the 16th play of the drive. Houghtlin came in, with backup quarterback Mark Vlasic serving as his holder. Schembechler called a time-out, trying to add pressure to the kick. Houghtlin still booted the ball perfectly, and chaos erupted.

Players and fans piled on Houghtlin and Vlasic in the mdidle of the field.

"When I was in the middle of that pileup, I was worried about getting killed — really," Houghtlin said.[2]

"We piled on the kicker and the holder, and he [Vlasic] was suffocating on the bottom," Long said. "It's funny now, but it was a scary scene. Everybody was piling on him and all the fans came out. It was just an unbelievable scene. It was a huge win for us and I've never seen Hayden Fry happier."

Iowa had the No. 1 offense in America, and the Hawkeyes didn't slow down much against Michigan. Long completed 26 of 39 passes for 297 yards. Harmon rushed for 120 yards in 32 carries and caught six passes for 72 yards.

Meanwhile, Michigan's Jim Harbaugh didn't have much luck through the air. He completed 8 of 13 passes for 55 yards and one touchdown, a six-yard pass to fullback Gerald White.

Michigan led, 7–6, at halftime. Iowa (6-0) regained the lead at 9–7 with 14:20 left on Houghtlin's 36-yard field goal. Then Michigan's Mike Gillette connected on a 40-yard field goal to put the Wolverines on top, 10–9, with 10:55 remaining.

When Houghtlin was way short on a 44-yard field-goal try with 7:38 to play, Iowa fans sensed trouble. But Michigan (5-1) could not move the ball, giving Houghtlin a chance to win the game.

"Probably of all my games in my college career, that was the one that stood out," said Long.

Postscript: Iowa won the Big Ten title despite losing to Ohio State later in the year. The Hawkeyes finished 10-2 and ranked tenth by the Associated Press after they were beaten by UCLA, 45–28, in the Rose Bowl. Long ended up third nationally in passing efficiency and threw for 2,978 yards and 26 touchdowns. He finished with more than 10,000 passing yards in his career. He was runner-up to Auburn running back Bo Jackson for the Heisman Trophy in the closest race in the award's history. Long was a 1986 first-round draft choice of the Detroit Lions.

Michigan beat Nebraska, 27–23, in the Fiesta Bowl to finish 10-1-1. The Wolverines ended up No. 2 behind national champion Oklahoma. Harbaugh led the nation in passing efficiency and completed 65.6 percent of his passes for 1,913 yards and 18 touchdowns. Schembechler retired at the end of the 1989 season. He had a 234-65-8 record in 27 years of coaching, the last 22 years at Michigan.

References

1. Iowa Sports Information Department, 19 October 1985.
2. Ibid.

Penn State Grounds Testaverde
Penn State 14, Miami 10 • January 2, 1987

For 59 minutes, Penn State played an inspired and ferocious defense in assuming a four-point lead against Miami before an overflow crowd of 73,098 in the Fiesta Bowl in Tempe, Arizona. But with one minute remaining, that effort seemed in jeopardy of being wasted.

Miami, the No. 1–ranked team, had the ball on Penn State's ten-yard line. It was first and goal with the national championship on the line.

Facing the top quarterback in the country in Miami's Heisman Trophy winner Vinny Testaverde, the Nittany Lions were trying desperately to hold on against a team that had scored only 10 points up to that point but had averaged 38 during the season.

And the second-ranked Nittany Lions were up to the task.

After three plays left Miami on Penn State's 13, Testaverde fired a pass downfield that was intercepted by right inside linebacker Pete Giftopoulos at the one-yard line—the fifth time that Testaverde had thrown an interception in the game. The interception sewed up Penn State's 14–10 victory and marked the first time all season that Miami's high-flying offense had been grounded.

Miami (11-1) totaled 445 yards, 285 by the pass, but could push across only one touchdown and a field goal. Miami had not been held to less than 23 points in any game during the season and had scored 34 or more in eight games.

"I feel pretty good about our offensive team," Miami Coach Jimmy Johnson said afterward. "Most times when we hit the field, we're going to be able to score more than 10 points.

"But Penn State just has a great defensive team. They've given up only 10 or 11 points a game. They not only did a great job tonight, they've done a great job all year long."[1]

It was the second consecutive season Penn State had a chance of winning the national title in a bowl game. In the 1986 Orange Bowl, the Nittany Lions lost their No. 1 rating when they were steamrolled by Oklahoma, 25–10.

It was a different story against Miami.

This time it was Penn State's opponent that would be held to ten points.

"Our defense played about as well as I've ever seen a college football team play defense," said Penn State Coach Joe Paterno, whose team improved to 12-0.[2]

Still, Paterno conceded that his team faced disaster and a definite momentum shift after Johnson made good on a stunning fourth-down gamble. With fourth and six and the ball at the Miami 27 with 2:24 remaining, Johnson disdained the punt and had Testaverde crank up his right arm again.

Penn State Coach Joe Paterno. (Photo courtesy of Penn State Sports Information Department.)

And when Testaverde completed a pass to Brian Blades for a 31-yard gain, Paterno admitted to being worried.

"In my experience," Paterno said, "whenever I've taken a big, big gamble like that and made it, I've usually won. The kids get to thinking, 'Look out, this must be our night.' And everything starts to happen. I was scared."[3]

His concern increased when Testaverde drove Miami to the ten-yard line with 1:01 remaining. But then Penn State's defense stiffened.

After Testaverde completed a pass for five yards, he was sacked for an eight-yard loss. It was now third and thirteen. Testaverde then tried another pass across the field to halfback Warren Williams but it fell incomplete.

Penn State tailback D. J. Dozier.

Then came fourth down and Giftopoulos' second interception of the game.

"[Testaverde] has a tendency to look to the area where he was going to throw," Giftopoulos said. "On that last play, he was looking right at that spot from the time the ball was snapped. All I had to do was follow his eyes. He threw the ball right to me."[4]

Miami's three consecutive passes after reaching Penn State's five surprised most people. The Hurricanes still had two time-outs remaining and the fleet Alonzo Highsmith was in vintage form.

But Highsmith, who rushed for 119 yards in 18 carries, was passed up in favor of Testaverde's passing.

Johnson, in fact, had wanted to run on second down. So did offensive coordinator Gary Stevens. But Testaverde voted to pass and got his wish, but not the result he desired.

Defense paved the way for Penn State's decisive score in the second quarter. Shane Conlan, Penn State's All-American outside linebacker, picked off a Testaverde pass, returning the ball 38 yards to the Miami five.

Two plays later, tailback D. J. Dozier, who gained 99 yards in 20 carries, raced six yards up the middle for the touchdown that gave Penn State a 14–10 lead.

Penn State would not score thereafter, but the Nittany Lions' defense also would take the wind out of the sails of the Hurricanes' offense.

Postscript: Penn State finished as the No. 1 team, the second time in five seasons the Nittany Lions had earned the honor. Miami finished No. 2.

Testaverde completed 63.4 percent of his passes his senior season for 2,057 yards and 26 touchdowns. In his career, Testaverde passed for 6,058 yards and 48 touchdowns with 25 interceptions.

Testaverde was the No. 1 player chosen in the 1987 National Football League draft when he was selected by the Tampa Bay Buccaneers. He became a starter for the Buccaneers late in his rookie season and finished with 1,081 yards passing that season.

References

1. *Los Angeles Times*, 3 January 1987.
2. Ibid.
3. *Sports Illustrated*, 9 January 1987.
4. *Los Angeles Times*, 3 January 1987.

Notre Dame Survives Brawl with Miami

Notre Dame 31, Miami 30 • October 15, 1988

Imagine a heavyweight championship bout in which the two combatants slug it out in the middle of the ring from start to finish, each refusing to back down. Then, in the 15th round, the one left standing is declared the winner.

Notre Dame linebacker Frank Stams. (Courtesy of Notre Dame Sports Information Department.)

That's pretty much how the Notre Dame–Miami game went. Before the game even started, there was a brawl between the teams. Then the battle began with each team trading its best punches. Finally, these two unbeaten teams decided the winner with a single play in the final minute.

Miami scored a touchdown on quarterback Steve Walsh's 11-yard, fourth-down pass to Andre Brown to close within 31–30 with 45 seconds remaining. The Hurricanes elected to go for a two-point conversion.

The sellout crowd of 59,075 at Notre Dame Stadium was on its feet. Victory or defeat would be decided by the success or failure of this one play.

"People always ask, 'What happened in the huddle?'" Notre Dame linebacker Frank Stams said in 1991. "I said, 'Nobody said anything.'

Notre Dame defensive back Pat Terrell.

They asked why. I said, 'Well, everybody was praying they weren't coming their way.'"

As it turned out, Miami came toward safety Pat Terrell, who batted down a Walsh pass to Leonard Conley in the end zone. The Irish had beaten top-ranked Miami, 31–30, ending the Hurricanes' 36-game regular-season winning streak.

"Everybody kind of hung together and at that point in the game, more than any other time, we played as a total defensive unit," Stams said. "Nobody panicked. I felt we deserved to win."

Miami, however, had plenty to complain about. The Hurricanes had seven turnovers, including a controversial fumble on Notre Dame's one-yard line. Walsh had three interceptions in losing for the first time in 17 games as a starter. He completed 31 of 50 passes for 424 yards and four touchdowns.

It was a wild, emotional game, one that started before the opening kickoff when Miami players tangled with their counterparts in a tunnel.

"We were coming off the field and for some reason, the Miami players were stalled in the tunnel," Stams said. "We're trying to make our way through and a few tempers flared. As soon as the fight broke out, I figured I was going to do enough fighting on the field, so I put my helmut on and went the other way.

"I'm a lover, not a fighter. I noticed a lot of freshmen and sophomores up front fighting."

Thus the atmosphere of a prize fight had been created, and the teams went after each other with little trepidation.

After a 7–7 tie early in the second quarter, Notre Dame went on top, 21–7, as Braxston Banks caught a nine-yard touchdown pass from quarterback Tony Rice and Terrell returned a Walsh interception 60 yards for a touchdown.

Walsh recovered brilliantly, throwing a 23-yard touchdown pass to Conley on fourth and five and adding a 15-yard touchdown pass to running back Cleveland Gary, making the score 21–21 at halftime.

In the third quarter, Rice threw an interception, but on Miami's first play in possession, Conley lost the ball on a fumble. Then Notre Dame's Bill Hackett had a 43-yard field goal attempt blocked. Later, Miami tried a fake punt that failed. No one was holding back in a nerve-wracking final 30 minutes.

Rice teamed with Ricky Watters on a 44-yard pass play and Pat Eilers ran in from the two to give Notre Dame a 28–21 lead. Then Walsh threw another interception, setting up a Notre Dame field goal and a 31–21 Irish lead. Miami closed to 31–24 on a 23-yard field goal by Carlos Huerta to start the fourth quarter.

With seven minutes remaining, the game's most controversial play occurred. On fourth and seven at the Notre Dame 11, Walsh completed a short pass to Gary, who lost the ball at the Notre Dame one. Notre Dame's Michael Stonebreaker recovered.

Miami believed that Gary had lost the ball after he crossed the goal line. "I broke the plane," Gary said afterward. "I know I did. But when they told me it [the fumble] was a dead ball, I figure, 'Great, we've got the ball on the one.' But the next thing I know, their offense is lining up across from us."[1]

The officials ruled Gary had fumbled, giving the ball to Notre Dame.

The next year, Gary and Stams became teammates on the Los Angeles Rams, and the two expressed differing opinions about the play.

"He brings up the fumble and I tell him, 'Cleveland, you got to hold

Notre Dame Coach Lou Holtz. (Photo courtesy of Notre Dame Sports Information Department.)

190   Notre Dame 31, Miami 30 (1988)

onto the ball.' I believe it was a fumble; he doesn't think it was," Stams said.

Miami Coach Jimmy Johnson didn't agree with the officials' decision, but he said the game "shouldn't have come down to that. There were just too many mistakes, a ton of them. Although in my mind we still should have won."[2]

Notre Dame certainly had the advantage in emotional incentive. Notre Dame Coach Lou Holtz didn't need to remind his players that they had lost four consecutive times to the Hurricanes, including an embarrassing 58-7 defeat in 1985.

Stams had been winless against the Hurricanes until the one-point victory. "Every time I bring up that game, Cleveland brings up the three other games they beat us," Stams said.

But Stams admitted the Hurricanes earned plenty of respect. "I took that victory and got out of Dodge," he said. "It was my fourth time trying to beat those guys. Of all the teams we played year after year, that was the only team we had never beaten.

"What made them so difficult was they had fine coaching and great players. And the pro-style offense they ran really made them a threat, along with their speed."

An unsung hero for the Fighting Irish was Rice. Known more for his running skills, Rice finished with 195 yards passing.

Postscript: As great as the game was, it became the No. 2 story in most sports sections across the country the next day. On the same day as the Miami–Notre Dame game, Kirk Gibson hit a dramatic, two-out, two-run, pinch-hit home run in the bottom of the ninth inning to give the Los Angeles Dodgers a 3–2 victory over the Oakland Athletics in Game 1 of the 1988 World Series.

Notre Dame's win over Miami improved its record to 6-0. The Irish went on to beat West Virginia, 34–21, in the Fiesta Bowl, to finish 12-0 and win the national championship.

Miami dropped to 5-1 with the defeat but didn't lose another game, going 11-1 while beating Nebraska 23-3, in the Orange Bowl. The Hurricanes finished No. 2. Johnson resigned at the end of the season to become head coach of the Dallas Cowboys.

Miami's Gary and defensive end Bill Hawkins were first-round draft choices of the Los Angeles Rams in 1989. Walsh, fourth in the Heisman Trophy balloting, was picked by the Dallas Cowboys in the supplemental draft.

Stams was drafted in the second round by the Rams. Terrell became a second-round pick of the Rams in 1990, meaning that four players from that 1988 Miami–Notre Dame game became teammates on the Rams.

References

1. *Los Angeles Times*, 16 October 1988.
2. Ibid.

Amazing Drive Propels Miami

Miami 27, Notre Dame 10 • November 25, 1989

Don't blame Notre Dame players if they regard Miami's Orange Bowl as one of their least favorite places to visit.

"I hate this damn place," Notre Dame linebacker Ned Bolcar said after the top-ranked Fighting Irish had its 23-game winning streak end with a 27–10 loss to Miami in a regular-season finale.[1]

It was the fifth time in the 1980s that Notre Dame had come to the Orange Bowl and lost. And, as Bolcar said, "This one is going to haunt us the rest of our lives."[2]

There was no more eerie feeling than watching Miami's offense stay on the field for almost 11 minutes in the third quarter. The Hurricanes ran off an incredible 22-play, 80-yard scoring drive that used 10:47. Counting losses and penalties, Miami gained 118 yards on the march. At one point, Miami faced a 3rd-and-44 situation and got the first down. When the quarter ended, Miami had increased a 17–10 halftime lead to 24–10.

"Killed us," Bolcar said of the drive.[3]

The drive was directed by quarterback Craig Erickson, and the crowd of 81,634 was mesmerized by its seemingly endless duration.

It began on the Miami 20 and ended 22 plays later with Erickson throwing a five-yard touchdown pass to Dale Dawkins on third and goal. In between, there were some unforgettable moments, none more startling than the 3rd-and-44 situation.

Miami Coach Dennis Erickson. (Photo courtesy of Miami Sports Information Department.)

On fourth and one from the Miami 39, fullback Stephen McGuire ran two yards for a first down. Soon, Miami was penalized 15 yards for a personal foul, and it was first and 25 from the 26. On the next play, Erickson lost the ball while fading back to pass. Notre Dame's Devon McDonald thought he recovered but fumbled it, and Miami took over 23 yards behind the line of scrimmage.

After a run picked up little yardage, the Hurricanes had their 3rd-and-44 situation from their seven-yard line. "We just ran four streaks up the football field," Miami Coach Dennis Erickson said in 1991.

Wide receiver Randal Hill got open, beating cornerback Stan Smagala and safety Pat Terrell, and Erickson hit him for a 44-yard gain. It was first down. An incredible drive continued. "Oh yes, that's our usual third-and-forty-four call," Dennis Erickson joked.

Craig Erickson had noticed that Terrell was slow getting over to provide support in covering the speedy Hill. "The free safety is on the hashes and our guy runs 40 yards in 4.35 seconds," Craig Erickson said. "He can get by most free safeties."[4]

"I guess I should have been deep," said Terrell.[5]

Coincidentally, the year before, Terrell batted down a potential game-winning, two-point conversion pass in the end zone that preserved Notre Dame's 31–30 victory over Miami.

So now Miami had a first down on the Notre Dame 49 and people were beginning to wonder if this drive was destined to succeed. Then came a couple more runs, a couple of completions and finally Erickson's five-yard touchdown pass to Dawkins that gave Miami (10-1) its 14-point lead. Notre Dame (11-1) was beaten.

What a win it was for Miami's two Ericksons, both of whom were trying to prove something. Craig Erickson was trying to follow in the footsteps of past Miami quarterback greats Bernie Kosar and Vinny Testaverde. And Dennis Erickson was in this first season after replacing Jimmy Johnson. Many had questioned whether the former Washington State coach could win big games. His new team had lost to rival Florida State earlier in the season.

"Do I feel relieved? About 3,000 pounds off my back," said Dennis Erickson afterward.[6]

In fact, the game was a crucial confidence builder for the Hurricanes. "It was real key because we had lost to Florida State," Dennis Erickson said. "Any time there are coaching changes, there are people who wonder about you as a coach in big games. It was a key win for the credibility of the coaching staff."

Important to the victory was Miami's defense, which did not allow Notre Dame to score an offensive touchdown. The Fighting Irish were held to a season-low 142 yards rushing.

"I can offer you a million excuses, but not a single reason," said Notre Dame Coach Lou Holtz afterward.[7]

Miami opened a 10–0 lead in the first quarter, including a 55-yard touchdown pass from Erickson to Dawkins that was made possible when Miami's line successfully blocked during a blitz.

Notre Dame tied the score at 10 with 2:08 left in the second quarter on Bolcar's 49-yard interception return for a touchdown. Then Miami took charge.

With 1:11 left before halftime, Notre Dame quarterback Tony Rice threw a pass that was intercepted by linebacker Bernard Clark, who

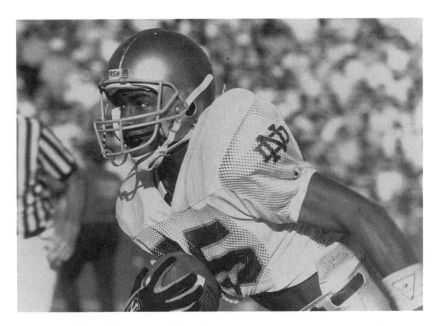

Notre Dame's Raghib Ismail. (Photo courtesy of Notre Dame Sports Information Department.)

returned the ball 50 yards to the Notre Dame eight. Three plays later, McGuire scored from the five for a 17–10 Miami advantage.

Erickson completed 16 of 26 passes for 210 yards. Rice was 7 of 15 for 106 yards and two interceptions. The explosive Raghib (Rocket) Ismail, Notre Dame's big-play weapon, was limited to 29 yards rushing in four carries.

Postscript: Miami won its third national championship in seven seasons, finishing 11-1 after beating Alabama, 33–25, in the Sugar Bowl. The Hurricanes had the No. 1 defense in the nation, allowing the fewest yards per game (216.5) and fewest points per game (9.3). The defensive line was led by All-Americans Greg Mark and Cortez Kennedy. Also playing was lineman Russell Maryland, later to become the 1990 Outland Trophy winner and first player taken in the 1991 National Football League draft by the Dallas Cowboys.

Notre Dame finished 12-1 and ranked No. 2. The Fighting Irish beat Colorado, 21–6, in the Orange Bowl. Rice placed fourth in the Heisman Trophy balloting.

References

1. *Los Angeles Times,* 26 November 1989.
2. Ibid.
3. Ibid.
4. Ibid.
5. Ibid.
6. Ibid.
7. Ibid.

Five Downs and a Cloud of Controversy

Colorado 33, Missouri 31 • October 6, 1990

It was one of the strangest and most controversial football games, one that was ultimately decided by the officials who admitted afterward that they had blundered.

Colorado scored the winning touchdown in its 33–31 victory over host Missouri as time expired. The score came shortly after the officials had erroneously given the Buffaloes an extra down.

"We'll never know how we let a down get away from us,"[1] referee J. C. Louderback said months later.

With 31 seconds remaining in the game, 12th-ranked Colorado trailed, 31–27, to lightly regarded Missouri. Colorado had a first and goal on Missouri's three-yard line.

Colorado quarterback Charles Johnson spiked the ball to stop the clock with 28 seconds left. On second down, Eric Bieniemy ran two yards to the one-yard line. Colorado called a time-out with 18 seconds left. Unnoticed was that the sideline down marker was not changed, and Colorado received another second down.

Bieniemy was halted for no gain. An official stopped the clock with eight seconds left, ruling Missouri was too slow unpiling. On what should have been fourth down (third according to the marker), Johnson spiked the ball to stop the clock with two seconds left. On fifth down (fourth according to the marker), Johnson scored from the one, although television replays failed to show conclusively that he had reached the end zone.

The final play produced a wild, chaotic scene. At first, none of the officials signaled for a touchdown, and many of the 46,856 fans thought Missouri had won the Big Eight opener. They charged onto the field to celebrate, tearing down the goal posts at the opposite end of the field. But soon the line judge signaled a touchdown, infuriating Missouri fans. Two were arrested and three others injured in the melee.

Twenty minutes after the game, Missouri Coach Bob Stull met with the officials trying to change the outcome, but the final, bizarre sequence of events stood. Under NCAA rules, once the fifth-down play was mistakenly run, nothing could be changed.

"It boggles the mind," Louderback remembered. "All the players, all the coaches, all the officials — not one person noticed. It will always be an amazing thing in my mind. How could it happen? And if it's going to happen, why must it happen in the last seconds of the last play that decides such an important game."[2]

The controversy surrounding the game's last 30 seconds overshadowed some splendid individual performances. Missouri quarterback Kent Kiefer completed 19 of 34 passes for 326 yards and three touchdowns. Bieniemy rushed for a career-high 217 yards in 29 carries.

Colorado improved to 4-1-1 and Missouri dropped to 2-3.

Postscript: The significance of Colorado's victory increased as the season progressed. In the end, Colorado beat Notre Dame, 10–9, in the Orange Bowl to win a share of the national championship, but the Buffaloes had to answer questions about whether their No. 1 ranking was tainted by the fifth-down controversy.

In fact, many questioned whether Colorado should have offered to forfeit the victory as Cornell did in a similar situation. In 1940, Cornell defeated Dartmouth, 7–3, on a fifth-down play and later surrendered its victory. Subsequently, NCAA rules were changed to prevent teams from forfeiting in similar situations. But an angry Colorado Coach Bill McCartney refused to even consider the idea. He believed his team would have routed Missouri if not for treacherous field conditions caused by the slippery OmniTurf. McCartney's lack of humility struck some as arrogance and caused a backlash against the Buffaloes.

"I get mail about it," McCartney said three months after the game. "Columns are still being written about that game. I get reminded all the

Colorado Coach Bill McCartney. (Photo courtesy of Colorado Sports Information Department.)

time. I'm not going to ignore it. I'm not going to duck it. I felt strongly that Colorado earned the victory and does not apologize for the victory."[3]

"We're not going to give up the victory just so some old lady can say, 'Oh, they're so nice," said Colorado kicker Jim Harper in 1991. "I feel we got cheated a little bit because if we played on a good field, we would have blown them away by 50 points. It was so frustrating to watch Eric Bieniemy go to the outside with 40 yards of open room in front of him and then slip and fall."

"I don't think we should have given the victory back," said

Colorado tight end Sean Brown in 1991. "It wasn't our fault. It wasn't their [Missouri's] fault. It was the referees who made the mistake."

Missouri appealed the outcome to the Big Eight Conference, which allowed the score to stand but suspended the seven officials. Louderback, who received hate mail, retired at the end of the season. To make sure his team did not encounter a similar situation, McCartney assigned a person to keep track of the downs.

Postscript: After defeating Notre Dame in the Orange Bowl to finish 11-1-1, Colorado was named the national champion by the Associated Press. Georgia Tech was selected the national champion by United Press International.

Coincidentally, Colorado's victory in the Orange Bowl was influenced by another critical call by the officials. Notre Dame's Raghib Ismail returned a punt 91 yards for an apparent game-winning touchdown in the final minute, but it was nullified because of a clipping penalty.

Missouri finished the season 4-7.

References

1. The Associated Press, 2 January 1991.
2. Ibid.
3. *The National,* 26 December 1990.

Bibliography

Alabama 1990 Football Press Guide.

The Associated Press.

Brown, Gene, ed. *The New York Times Scrapbook Encyclopedia of Sports History — The Complete Book of Football.* Indianapolis/New York: Bobbs-Merrill Company, Inc., 1980.

Claassen, Harold. *Football's Unforgettable Games.* New York: Ronald Press Company, 1963.

Eubanks, Lon. *The Fighting Illini — A Story of Illinois Football.* Huntsville, AL: The Strode Publishers, Inc., 1976.

Hyman, Mervin D. and Gordon S. White, Jr. *Big Ten Football, Its Life and Times, Great Coaches, Players, and Games.* New York: Macmillan Publishing Company, 1977.

Los Angeles Times.

McCallum, John. *Ivy League Football Since 1872.* New York: Stein and Day Publishers, 1977.

Meserole, Mike, ed. *The 1990 Information Please Sports Almanac.* Boston: Houghton Mifflin Company.

The National. (All sports newspaper no longer in publication.)

The New York Times.

Notre Dame 1990 Football Press Guide.

Porter, David L., ed. *Biographical Dictionary of American Sports: Football.* New York: Greenwood Press, 1987.

Smith, Don R. *Official Encyclopedia of Football.* New York: W. H. Smith Publishers, Inc., 1989.

The Sporting News.

Sports Illustrated.

Texas Christian 1990 Football Press Guide.

United Press International.

The Washington Post.

Index

DATE DUE
